Living Free
Like You're 3!

Alicia V. Sharpe

ISBN: 0615860656
ISBN-13: 978-0615860657
Copyright © 2013 Alicia V. Sharpe
All rights reserved.

For my amazing children. God has changed my life so much with each one of you. You have lived this book out and have truly shown me the amazing love of Christ in my life like no one else could. I love you so much and I'm looking forward to all that God has in store for each one of you.

Table of Contents

ACKNOWLEDGMENTS

I want to thank, first and foremost, Jesus. He is a friend like no other and has met me so many ways through the writing of this book. There truly is no one like Him. I would also like to thank my amazing husband, Chris. Your love and support have encouraged me beyond measure to continue to pursue all the dreams of my heart, including this one. Thanks also to my friend and author William Stadler for your invaluable input, encouragement, and great wisdom on the many different levels throughout this project. I also want to thank my dear friend, Kara Hensley for reading and completeing some final editing touches in preparation for publishing. Thank you also to so many supportive friends and family as many hours have been put into the writing and publishing of this book.

PREFACE

Never in a million years would I have thought I'd be writing a preface to a book that I had the privilege of writing. When God placed a dream in my heart many years ago with this idea of living like a child, it's been on my mind and heart ever since. Every time I'd look at a child, I'd see the traits that Jesus was talking about when He said to "become like a little child." I'd watch my kids closely, noticing the innocence and amazing love they display, not to mention all the fun they have in life. It made me realize how precious this life really is, and that God loves us so much. He loves us so much!!

I knew it was time to move forward with writing this book when I was truly set free in my heart from so much of the bondage that had been holding me back. Even as a vocational minister, my daily life and my heart did not display what I knew Jesus was talking about when He said we would live an abundant life. I was miserable, but through an amazing process, I finally realized by God's grace who I am in Christ and that no matter what I do in this life, His love for me will never fail. Never. It's not about me at all…it's all about Him. His great big love for me. His desire is to see me live a life of greatness empowered to live out all that He has shown us in the Bible. And no matter what you've been told before, it IS possible.

Living life as a Christian is so exciting. You never know what God will do next…if you only believe. Children understand that principle with no question. They believe, wonder, ask, love, and forgive like no other. No wonder Jesus said we should live like that.

My prayer is that you will be encouraged as you read as well as challenged to just live life with a "go for it" attitude. I mean, what do you have to lose? Be who

God has made you to be. God is faithful. He loves you...Choose to live like you're 3 everyday and you'll see amazing things unfold before your eyes!

Part 1

Free to be Fabulous!

The sermon I think this Mom will never forget.... this particular Sunday sermon... "Dear Lord," the minister began, with arms extended toward heaven and a rapturous look on his upturned face. "Without you, we are but dust." He would have continued but at that moment my very obedient daughter who was listening leaned over to me and asked quite audibly in her shrill little girl voice, "Mom, what is butt dust?"
(www.HeardonthePlayground.com)

My 5 year old John came running up so thrilled and out of breath, "Mom, mom, watch! I can count in Spanish with my EYES CLOSED!"

I went on a date with my 4 year old son. I thought it would be good to teach him how to be a gentleman. I gave him money to pay for our date and explained what kinds of things gentlemen do (open doors, pay for the date, etc.). As we leave the car he says with a serious look on his face, "Man mom, being a gentleman is really hard work!"

Chapter 1

Free to be Beautiful

I was having a chat with my 8 year old son about how it is nice to think about other people first... he looked at me and said, "But why Mommy, I like me. I am one of the best people I know." I guess the self-confidence talk is not really needed right now."

"God made me. He made me sooo beautiful! And He made chocolate milk!" These are the words from a 3 year old little girl, and they are so true! God made you beautiful, and there is nothing else you can do to be more beautiful in God's sight. The question is, "Do you really believe it?"

When I look at my kids, they have no doubt that they are amazing. They know it. I ask both of my daughters regularly, "Do you know that you are beautiful?" Without hesitation they answer, "Yes!" I ask, "Are you gorgeous?" They say, "Yes, mommy, I'm gorgeous, and so are you!"

Kids seem to inherently know these things. They know that they are amazing and valuable. They know that they are beautiful, and my son, without a doubt, knows he's handsome and strong. They know that they have a purpose and a destiny in life, and they are not afraid to say it. It's interesting for me to observe this confidence in all of my children and with other children as well.

They are absolutely right. They are beautiful. I am beautiful. You are beautiful. I didn't always believe it though. When in life was it that I started questioning my beauty and my value? When did I start thinking that I was the one who was left out and that I'm not as beautiful as everyone else around me? Who told me that I don't measure up and that I am not amazing? When exactly in the course of my life did I start to think that I'm not both valuable and priceless? Maybe for you this hasn't been an issue. Maybe you've always known of your beauty, but that was not the case for me.

My "Beautiful" Story

The title of this chapter has been something that I longed to be for so many years. Free to be beautiful. Those words, free and beautiful, mean so much to me. Knowing deep in my heart that I am free and beautiful has always been a challenge. I've known it in my mind, but for me to grasp this truth in my heart has taken quite a while. It wasn't until recently, in my mid-30's, that I started believing it. Or maybe I should say, believing it *again* and *living* as if I believed it.

I came from a great family, but no one ever told me that I was a princess, so I lost that perception at a very early age. I hated to do anything "girly," and the closest thing that I ever had to dolls were stuffed animals. I would play outside all the time with my older brother. We'd play baseball, football, and anything else we could do outdoors. I was definitely considered a "tomboy," and that was fine with me. Don't get me wrong, you can definitely be a "tomboy princess" and know you're beautiful, but that wasn't my story.

When I was around 8 years old I decided to get my hair cut short. For most of my life at that point I had beautiful, long blond hair, but I didn't want it that way anymore. I remember one day walking home after getting off the bus and a man who I met on the way home said something that I still remember to this day. It was unintentional, but the words that came out of his mouth implied that he thought I was a little boy. This took me aback, and I remember it cutting my heart deeply. Something so simple changed the way I viewed myself. I was self-conscious about the way I looked after that, even at such a young age.

Just before I went to Junior High school my dad got a promotion with his job, and we ended up leaving all of my friends in West Virginia and moving to Fayetteville, North Carolina. My mom tried to convince my brother and me that it was going to be great. She would say, "Just think, you'll only be 2 hours away from the beach!" If you knew me back then I was very shy and didn't say much at all. I wasn't too excited about the idea because I would be leaving the comfort of all my friends and everything I knew.

I still had short hair when we moved, and I never thought it looked very good. I was already worried about the way I looked because I had so many pimples all over my face and didn't like what I saw in the mirror. I'll never forget the day I thought that my bangs were too long. It was simple, I'd just take the scissors and cut a little bit off of them and make it all better. So I got the scissors and went up to the bathroom to trim my hair. Little did I know that if you cut your hair when it's wet, it will not be as long when it dries! Well, as you probably figured out, I cut them way too short, and my hair looked terrible! What made it even worse was that school pictures were happening that day. Needless to say we did *not* purchase those!

My mom and dad were not the type to be very affectionate. I knew that they loved me, but they weren't very verbal in telling me things that little girls like to hear. I didn't know that I was a princess. I didn't know that I was beautiful. I never really thought about it. I never got up in my daddy's lap and sat there while those words were spoken into my life. Instead, I was out on the softball field while my dad coached. He would always throw the ball with me as I was growing up, and that's where I felt loved by him.

As I grew up and became a woman, I never fully grasped what it meant to be beautiful. I had defined myself as a tomboy because I was good at sports and things like that, and that's who the world saw me as. I didn't realize you could be both. I wanted to do what I could do best to receive the love and acceptance that I needed, so I played the part that others thought I should play, and when I excelled in these areas, I gained acceptance.

I went through a season - many years really- after having kids where I was miserable. It was during the time when my children were very young. I was in my late twenties to early thirties, and I was upset most of the time. I was never happy, and honestly, I never thought I measured up to a standard the world had placed on me. I didn't like the way I looked or acted, and I didn't truly realize that I was beautiful or valuable. I didn't know who God had made me to be. I constantly thought I was a failure in life and that I didn't deserve love.

God took me through a healing process over those years, which I will explain in more detail later, and because of it, I am a new person. Knowing that I'm beautiful and that Jesus has set me free has changed my life! It's almost as if I was born again, again! Not caring what others think about me gives me confidence to be the beautiful me that God created. I am no longer trying to live up to others' expectations or to be anyone else. My audience is God alone.

Created in the Image of God

I mention these stories because image is something that we deal with for our entire lives. It doesn't matter what you're doing, where you are, or what you look like, the enemy doesn't want you to like who you are. He wants you to be so caught up in self condemnation and self hate that you'll be paralyzed and not go after the dreams that God has placed in your heart. He wants you to feel so badly about yourself that you're too ashamed even to go to God. The enemy wants to keep you in bondage at any cost.

If you really think about it, it makes no *logical* sense not to realize and recognize your value, even if you don't believe in God. Sure, we live in a huge world with 7 billion people so it might feel very easy to be overlooked or unimportant. The remarkable thing is that there is no one else in this great big world like you. Not one person. There are no duplicates. Nobody else shares the same vision, purpose, and destiny as you do. You even have your own fingerprint! God made you unique and valuable. He made you in His image and you are beautiful and amazing, and THAT is the truth. Anything else that we hear to contradict this is a lie. God formed you in your mother's womb and fashioned you to be exactly who you are. Psalm 139:13-14 says,

> *"For you created my inmost being; you knit me together in my mother's womb. I praise*

you because I am fearfully and wonderfully made; your works are wonderful, I know that full well."

Nobody that God made is a surprise, mistake, or an accident. We were all formed by Him and for Him.

Somewhere over the years we've allowed others to tell us who we are. We've let the captain of the cheerleading team tell us that we don't look as good as she does. Well, maybe she didn't actually *tell* us that, we just assumed it to be true. We've let someone in our family inform us that we'll never amount to anything. We've believed the lie that we can't accomplish our dreams and goals in our lives because we just don't have the gifts and talents to do what it takes. After all, we're just not as good as she is, or we're not as smart, or as fast, or as skinny. I mean, you simply can't be beautiful if you're overweight, right? Of course you can! You are beautiful, no matter what you weigh or what you think you see in the mirror. These are all lies from the enemy to get you to question who you really are at your core.

Weight and body image are so important in most women's lives – to the point that so much of what we do, think about and even our level of confidence revolves around what we look like on the outside. Some of us might feel like we're too big, while others might feel just the opposite. Maybe we have a skin tone that's not "ideal" or some other feature we don't like that makes us feel as if we're not beautiful. Maybe we're too tall, maybe too short...and the list goes on. If this isn't straight from the pit of hell I don't know what is.

How do we go from being innocent children, loving every part of who we are, to despising to even look at ourselves in the mirror? We are the same now as we were as children. Sure, a lot might have happened in your life over the course of the years, but if you are a creation of the Most High God (and we all are!), you are beautiful. You are amazing. You are exceptional.

You have been made in the image of God, and He is perfectly in love with you. He made you to be you, and no one else. He is the one who defines who you are, if you allow Him to. He is the one who took the time to think about you and create you...every single part of you. He is the one who loves you just the way you are, and He is all that matters.

We all need to ask God for the strength to believe that what He said about us is absolutely true and live our lives according to it. We must choose to stop believing the lies from the enemy. It's refreshing to look in the mirror and LOVE what I see. It's nice to walk around knowing that I am a gift from God and a blessing to others around me. It's nice to know that what I have to say and what I feel IS important and God put it in me for a reason. It's refreshing to know that I am alive on this earth for a reason...not to struggle or be in fear all the time, but to know that God's gifts and call for my life are irrevocable. (Romans 11:29)

Living life to only please God is so much better and more freeing than always living under the fear of man, or being overly concerned about what people think of me. When I think back to my teenage years, I realize how ridiculous it was to always worry about what someone thought of me. This seemed to bleed right on into the college years and even into adulthood. Why does it matter what everyone else thinks? Why do we care so much about what someone believes about us when the Creator of the entire universe is so passionately enthralled by us? If He thinks I'm wonderful, who am I not to think the same way?

Beautiful Defined

So, what does it look like to be beautiful and know that you're beautiful? I guess this is where we can turn to our 3 year-old mentors to help us out.

Young children don't try to be or to look like anyone but who they are. They embrace being a child. Sure, they might have fun and put on mommy or daddy's clothes or shoes, but they are completely satisfied in being who God made them to be. They are not unhappy with the way they appear at all.

The word "beautiful" in one dictionary is defined as: "The quality that gives intense pleasure to the sight or other senses."[1]

The Koine Greek word for beautiful was derived from the word that meant "hour;" thus beauty was associated with being of one's hour. A ripe fruit (of its time) was considered to be beautiful, whereas a young woman trying to appear older or an older woman trying to appear younger would not be considered beautiful.[2]

I love that definition! If you look around us today, so many people are trying to look a certain way, striving to please those around them and not fully embracing who God has made them to be. They've accepted the world's definition of beauty, and they're doing everything in their power to put themselves in the same mold as everyone else around them. Women color their hair, use wrinkle creams, and purchase millions of dollars of products that will keep them looking younger. Teenagers and young adults try to look older by wearing lots of make-up and acting a certain way to appear as someone whom they are not. I'm not saying that any of these products are necessarily wrong to use, but it's the heart behind using them that could make you question your true beauty.

This definition of beautiful hammers home a strong point. Being who you are, "in your hour," and not trying to appear as something else is true beauty. True beauty is knowing that you are enough just the way you are. True beauty is knowing that when you roll out of bed first thing in the morning, you're beautiful. True beauty is being confident in the way you look, dress, and even how gray your hair might be. It's okay, because that's who you are, and you are beautiful just the way God made you to be. If you're 45 and you have gray hair, then your appearance is "in your hour." That's how you're supposed to look. Knowing in your heart that you're beautiful even without makeup, hair color, or any product to alter your appearance, is priceless.

It is absolutely possible to love what you see in the mirror. It is possible in Christ to be free from the bondage of appearance and to know that you have what it takes. You can walk in freedom and confidence in this part of your life. You completely can. It is a lie for you to think that you are stuck the way you are. If the Son has set you free, you are free, indeed! Free to be beautiful. Free to love you.

The bottom line is this: knowing you're beautiful takes work. It's a full-on attack from the enemy against your identity and it takes a fight. The great thing is that God always wins. And as His child, you always win. The more you know the scripture that tells you of your beauty and of His beauty, the more you will believe it. The more time you spend letting God love you and just simply being in His presence, the more you will know what He says about you. You are a masterpiece, created in the image of God. There is no one else like you, and you are gorgeous. What a treasure God made when He made you!

So the next time you look at yourself in the mirror, make a choice to see what God sees. Choose to know what a three year old knows...you are incredibly beautiful. Just the way you are!

My daughter came home crying one day. Her friend's dog had gotten run over by a car. "He didn't suffer though," she said, "he died constantly."

JACK (age 3) was watching his Mom breast-feeding his new baby sister. After a while he asked: "Mom why have you got two? Is one for hot and one for cold milk?" (Heardontheplayground.com)

I was trying on a new color lipstick I just bought and was feeling pretty good about it. That was until my daughter walked over and said "Wow Mommy, I love your new Halloween makeup." (Heardontheplayground.com)

Chapter 2

Free to be Me

A friend of ours has a son who has been potty training. After coming home from a friend's house, the dad asked his son where his underwear were. He said that he had an accident and left his underwear at their house. When asking him where they were in the house, the boy said, "Don't worry, Dad! I hid them real good!" The friends have yet to find the underwear.

Control. Can I be totally honest? I always want to be in control and know what's coming next, however, I never really want to have the responsibility of being in control. That's a big task. Kids are so great because they don't know what the need for control is. They relax and let someone else be in charge...and that's okay. Sure, there is someone who should be in charge, but they are okay not being the one. They are just fine allowing their parents take them from place to place, feeding them food that they may or may not want to eat, and living wherever they are placed. If that's not freedom, I don't know what is. You might think that they don't have freedom to make decisions, but I guess you can look at it the other way—they are free to not have to make decisions.

Control can be a good thing or a bad thing, depending on how you relate with it. I know, unfortunately, that I have the tendency to try to control everyone in my family—after all, mommy knows best, right? Well, maybe not. Jesus knows best, and unless I'm completely submitted to His Lordship, my control will not be what He desires. I might do an average job getting things to run smoothly (doing things MY way, course), but not nearly as smoothly as the King of kings. He's the rock and the perfect leader. He's the one who knows the future, not me. Letting go and letting God can be difficult sometimes, but it's necessary.

The Shame, Fear, and Control Cycle

Control even spills over into who we are and who God made us to be. I've been a part of a ministry called "Restoring the Foundations (RTF)" and God, through this ministry, has literally changed my life. Something that is mentioned many times in RTF is a cycle called "shame, fear, and control."[3] Most of us deal with or have dealt with this cycle at one point in our lives. Some of us may perhaps have dealt with this for our entire lives. Let me explain it to you in further detail.

First of all there is shame. You feel ashamed for something you've done in the past or that is currently taking place in your life. Shame is the feeling within that you are hopelessly flawed and that something is wrong with you at your core. Shame is something that occurs in your life when you've done something or something was done to you that makes you feel embarrassed or again, flawed. Guilt, on the other hand, is "I did something bad." Shame is "I *am* bad." It strikes at your *identity*—who you are—not only your actions.

After shame comes fear. You are afraid that someone will find out about your flaws and who you are. You become afraid that they won't like you or accept you anymore. Fear paralyzes you from being honest with yourself as well as everyone else around you, including God. Then the control comes in. You try to take control of the situation by hiding. You don't allow anyone to see your heart because you know that it's flawed, and they won't accept you if they think you're flawed.[4] You do everything in your power to keep a wall up and keep others at a distance so you won't be exposed. This is exactly what Adam and Eve did. They ate the fruit and felt ashamed. Then they were afraid because of their sin, so they attempted to control the situation by hiding from God. Adam even tried to place the blame on Eve!

Here's a current example of this cycle to bring further clarity: Jane was sexually abused as a young child by her uncle. When her parents finally found out about the situation they dealt with it quietly and told Jane never to mention it to anyone. A deep root of shame began to grow in Jane, who of course, has kept silent about what happened for years. She is ashamed of her past and is scared what might happen if someone were to find out, so she keeps distance from anyone who tries to get too close.

Jane might never know the joy and fulfillment of a deep relationship. Her control is keeping her from spending intimate time with her friends, and even when she tries, she resists going deeper, fearing that her heart might be exposed. There is a façade on the outside, shielding her heart that that desperately longs to be free. She doesn't want someone to know what happened in the past. She tries to control the situation, and never allows anyone into her heart because of the fear that they would reject her and view her as flawed. Thoughts might even go through her head such as, "If she knew where I came from or what happened to me, she would never want to be my friend."

Jane also might be afraid to let go and have a good time in a situation, not because she doesn't want to participate, but because she doesn't want to look stupid in front of her friends. So, in turn, she doesn't even try letting go because she is controlling the situation by just not participating. Does Jane *have* to have a good time? Of course not. However, if Jane's refusal to enjoy herself comes from her shame and the fear of looking stupid, then clearly Jane is not free. She is bound by the shame in her soul.

This happens more than we know. We grew up a certain way, and since we've never fully dealt with some of the issues in our heart from the past, we're afraid of what others might think. Since we care about what others think, we'll do everything in our power to cover up what's really going on in our hearts. We might hide behind the façade of serving at the church so that everything appears to be great on the outside, but on the inside there is a lot of pain and disappointment. I know many families at church come with a happy face every week, but their home life isn't even close to what it appears to be on the outside.

Maybe things with your family or spouse aren't going too well, and you've been contemplating divorce. Maybe you have issues with your parents and don't want anyone to know. Maybe you're living in a world of debt. Burying these feelings and issues will not help you in any way. That simply is not freedom. God wants you to know that no matter where you are in life, He still loves you. No matter what you've done, there's nothing that the power of the blood of Jesus can't set you free from. The promise of Jesus is that He has set us free from all of our sin. Sin is no longer remembered in His sight so we become free when we are in Him. Sin no longer defines us, Christ does!

Living Under a False Identity

Many of us choose not to live in the freedom of whom God has made us to be. We live under a false identity that the enemy has convinced us of, and we define ourselves incorrectly while living a life of bondage because of it. It's as if we have been set free from prison, but we refuse to remove the handcuffs. God has so much more in store for our lives than this! We allow this shame and fear control our lives to the point that we won't even let God into our deepest parts, and we certainly will not open up to someone else. It is just like having a fake ID in your wallet, except it's in your heart instead. In the same way a fake ID is clearly not who we are, when we live under a false identity that anyone but the Lord has given us, we are living a lie.

I know for me, I dealt with this for a long time. I was afraid to participate in anything fun because I didn't want to look stupid. I was always afraid to minister in the church that we attended because there were so many ministers there that I felt were "better than me." That was simply untrue.

Singing is something that I have always loved to do, and I feel God's pleasure when I do it. When I was at this particular church I always felt like I never measured up. I'd sing on the worship team and feel like my gift wasn't good enough, so I withdrew. I didn't do as much of the things that I loved because I was told (by the devil, of course) that I couldn't do these things as well as others. In this form of control, I was held back not only from the joy of using my gifts but also from the joy of glorifying God through my gifts. I believed a lie. When I finally moved on from that church, these gifts that had become dormant, sprung to life. I felt confident to minister and sing again, and so I did just that. God was showing me that I couldn't let the fear of man or shame control my life anymore. I needed to just go for it and to trust God to minister through me while using the gifts that He had given me.

When I say free to be me that is exactly what I mean. You are free to be all of the wonderful things God has made you to be, paired with the amazing and unique flavor that He has given you.

What's great is that we all exhibit these traits through our different personalities and gifts that God has given to us. While all of us are called to live a free life in Christ and become more like Him, we are all different, and there is no one like you anywhere else in this world!

I love how God works like that. We're all so much the same, yet we're all so very different. Jesus didn't come to kill off who you are and make you a cookie-cutter Christian and act like everyone else. No! He came to empower you to become the REAL you. He came to set you free from all the shame and fear that holds you back from living a fun, peaceful, and fulfilling life in Christ. He didn't promise that it would be easy, but living in His promises is more fulfilling than anything else here on earth.

Free to be Me, not You!

Just as we need to live free in who we are in Christ, we need to encourage others to be free in who they are in Christ as well. Many of us are guilty of trying to enforce our convictions of how to live or how to "be" on someone else's life. I know that I have this tendency. Out of my heart to see someone grow in Christ, I try to make that person more like me instead of encouraging that person to be more like Christ. Or, instead of enforcing these convictions on someone's life, we choose to gossip about how they aren't living as "holy" as we are. I hate that! In Romans 14, Paul clearly says that this is not something we should be doing:

> *"Accept him whose faith is weak, without passing judgment on disputable matters. ² One man's faith allows him to eat everything, but another man, whose faith is weak, eats only vegetables. ³ The man who eats everything must not look down on him who does not, and the man who does not eat everything must not condemn the man who does, for God has accepted him. ⁴ Who are you to judge someone else's servant? To his own master he stands or falls. And he will stand, for the Lord is able to make him stand.⁵ One man considers one day more sacred than another; another man considers every day alike. Each one should be fully convinced in his own mind. ⁶ He who regards one day as special, does so to the Lord. He who eats meat, eats to the Lord, for he gives thanks to God; and he who abstains, does so to the Lord and gives thanks to God. ⁷ For none of us lives to himself alone and none of us dies to himself alone. ⁸ If we live, we live to the Lord; and if we die, we die to the Lord. So, whether we live or die, we belong to the Lord." (Romans 14:1-8, NIV)*

God has shown me through the years that many times who I think I am is not the truth of who I really am, or should I say, who He's made me to be. I've been brought up around people of all kinds who don't know

God. Based on what people told me and what people idolized, I created a definition of who I thought I was. Everything and everyone around me tells me how to believe and how to act based on their experiences and based on the values that society dictates. The problem with that, however, is that their way of viewing me or defining me is not who God has made me to be.

Many of us, especially the moms out there, spend so much of our lives serving others that we forget to look in the mirror and take care of who you see right in front of you. We neglect to take the time to find out who God has made us on the inside, so we allow others to tell us who we are. Sure you might be able to make it through the day, but there's no way, unless you spend quality time with Jesus, that your friendship with Him could be growing and thriving. We naturally become more like someone when we spend time with that person. If we consider Jesus to be the most important person to us, why do we continue to put off our one-on-one time with Him?

Finding Our True Identity

At the beginning of this chapter I mentioned how children become free by relinquishing control. Think with me for just a moment. It's God's job to guide our lives. He is our perfect parent. He guides us in the way we should go. He knows what's best for us. Just like a parent, God "trains us in the way we should go. (Prov. 22:6)" Whether we listen or not is up to us. Just like children, we must choose to give up our will and allow God to place His will within us. We allow God, not ourselves or others to define who we are...not just what we do or our calling, but who we are at our core. That's the hard part. When we have been living for so long as a "certain person," with a certain set of rules about what we will and won't do, allowing God to come in and clean us up can be challenging. But we MUST in order to grow. If we've closed the door on God, then we'll be stuck in a rut until we decide to let our go of our will. For some, that might not be until the day they die.

That's why it's so important to use the Bible, the amazing tool He's given to us. So many of us say we believe the Bible, but we don't have any idea what it says about who we are. Many of us say we believe what it says but haven't even read the entire Bible! We try to give to others out of what we've heard, but we never have had the revelation for ourselves.

This can be very problematic. Not only are we believing incorrectly about ourselves, we are trying to give others advice about something we don't know much about. It's important to build ourselves up by reading the Word and finding out what God says about who we are.

I've come to realize that children really know who they are, and the definition of who they are is straight from Jesus. As they get older and more of the ways of the world get injected into their thinking, this knowledge seem to fade. I've seen it in my children as they've gotten older. As we know who we are and are filled with and led by the Holy Spirit, His fruit naturally overflows from us. We truly can become free and live freely like a child again. Displaying His fruit is not something we strive to do, it comes as an overflow from being full of the Spirit and knowing who you are in Him.

When we're filled to overflowing with His love and power, nothing is impossible for us. We can be who GOD made us to be. We can live according to the Word of God. Being filled with the Spirit is something we need to ask God for everyday, and even multiple times throughout the day.

The "You" that God has made you to be is magnificent masterpiece. Period. If you think of yourself as anything less than that, you have the wrong perspective. You are just as important as anyone else on this planet. If you want to bless others and help them grow in their relationship with Christ, growth in your own life is required as well. You are worth taking care of. Time to yourself and with God is vitally important, and it is NOT selfish, despite what some might tell you. God is a jealous God, and He wants all of who He's made you to be, not just your leftovers. Think about some of the things God says you are. Say these out loud if you can.

> I am beautiful. (Yes, men, even you are
>   beautiful!) (Ps. 45:11)
> I am great. (Matt. 11:11)
> I am a child of the King. (1 John 3:1)
> I am loved. (1 John 3:1)
> I don't have a spirit of fear but of power, love,
>   and sound mind. (2 Tim. 1:7)
> I am the head and not the tail. (Deut. 28:13)
> I am God's masterpiece.(Eph. 2:10)
> His work in me will be completed. (Phil. 1:6)
> I am a new creation.(2 Cor. 5:17)

And those are just a few.

This story below is a great example of what God does for us. Even though we might know Him, He is constantly yearning to give us something more. Even though we settle for less than His best, He is patient with us. He has the best for us, if only we'll let go and grab hold of His heart for us!

The cheerful girl with bouncy golden curls was almost five. Waiting with her mother at the checkout stand, she saw them: a circle of glistening white pearls in a pink foil box. "Oh please, Mommy. Can I have them? Please, Mommy, please?"
Quickly the mother checked the back of the little foil box and then looked back into the pleading blue eyes of her little girl's upturned face. "A dollar ninety-five. That's almost $2.00. If you really want them, I'll think of some extra chores for you and in no time you can save enough money to buy them for you. Your birthday's only a week away and you might get another crisp dollar bill from Grandma."

As soon as Jenny got home, she emptied her penny bank and counted out 17 pennies. After dinner, she did more than her share of chores, and she went to the neighbor and asked Mrs. McJames if she could pick dandelions for ten cents.

On her birthday, Grandma did give her another new dollar bill, and at last she had enough money to buy the necklace.

Jenny loved her pearls. They made her feel dressed up and grown up. She wore them everywhere –
Sunday school, kindergarten, even to bed. The only time she took them off was when she went swimming or had a bubble bath. Mother said if they got wet, they might turn her neck green.
Jenny had a very loving daddy, and every night when she was ready for bed, he would stop whatever he was doing and come upstairs to read her a story. One night when he finished the story, he asked Jenny, "Do you love me?"

"Oh yes, Daddy. You know that I love you."

"Then give me your pearls."

"Oh, Daddy, not my pearls. But you can have Princess – the white horse from my collection. The one with the pink tail. Remember, Daddy? The one you gave me. She's my favorite."
"That's okay, Honey. Daddy loves you. Good night." And he brushed her cheek with a kiss.
About a week later, after the story time, Jenny's daddy asked again, "Do you love me?"

"Daddy, you know I love you."

"Then give me your pearls."

"Oh Daddy, not my pearls. But you can have my baby doll. The brand new one I got for my birthday. She is so beautiful and you can have the yellow blanket that matches her sleeper."

"That's okay. Sleep well. God bless you, little one. Daddy loves you," And as always, he brushed her cheek with a gentle kiss.

A few nights later when her daddy came in, Jenny was sitting on her bed with her legs crossed Indian-style. As he came close, he noticed her chin was trembling, and one silent tear rolled down her cheek. What is it, Jenny? What's the matter?"

Jenny didn't say anything but lifted her little hand up to her Daddy. And when she opened it, there was her little pearl necklace. With a little quiver, she finally said, "Here, Daddy. It's for you."

With tears gathering in his own eyes, Jenny's kind daddy reached out with one hand to take the dime-

store necklace, and with the other hand he reached into his pocket and pulled out a blue velvet case with a strand of genuine pearls and gave them to Jenny. He had them all the time. He was just waiting for her to give up the dime-store stuff so he could give her genuine treasure.

Jenny's father is like our heavenly Father. He also is waiting for us to give up our dime store stuff and seek Him first, so He can fling open the windows of Heaven and pour us out such a blessing that we will not have room enough to hold it.[5]

Just like Jenny held onto her fake pearls, we hold onto something that we're not. We cling to a specific fear or a definition of self that is not from the Lord, and we are terrified to let it go. We see the truth in the Word, and we still have a hard time believing what God says about us. Every word that came from God is absolutely true...even for you. You are great and amazing and loved more than you could ever imagine. Let go of your old thoughts, relinquish the control to Him, and embrace the truth about who you really are. Children do! They are free to be themselves, and what a glorious freedom it is!

I'm lying in my 4 year old's bed with him having one of those loving moments. I'm holding his little hand and telling him how proud I am of him for being good in school when he lovingly looked at me and says, "This is awkward."

My son and I were about to get on the elevator and all of a sudden he yelled, "Yeah, we get to ride the alligator." Elevator...alligator. Whatever.

BRITTANY (age 4) had an earache and wanted a pain killer. She tried in vain to take the lid off the bottle. Seeing her frustration, her Mom explained it was a child-proof cap and she'd have to open it for her. Eyes wide with wonder, the little girl asked: "How does it know it's me?

Chapter 3

Free to be Perfectly Imperfect

Our youngest son Ben was excited that he would soon turn six. My wife, so sad to have our baby grow up, asked him one day, "Oh, Ben, can't you stay five forever?"
"I can't Mom," he said with a serious look, "but I can act five forever." (HeardonthePlayground.com)

Kids are so encouraging to be around! Sure, they might have lots of melt downs (don't we all?), but overall, when you are around a 3 year old for any length of time you're going to find yourself laughing at some point. Children never cease to make you smile. They act like who they are, and say what they want to say…and it's priceless!

I was recently at my daughter's dance recital, and I have to be honest, my very favorite part of the recital, besides my daughter dancing of course, was when the little 3 year old princesses paraded on the stage. It was so cute. They were doing their very best to stay together with all their twirls and arm raises, but they simply could not. It really made me chuckle because they had no idea, nor did they care one bit that their performance wasn't "perfect." The thing was, it was absolutely perfect to me because they were being exactly who God made them to be—3 year olds. They had a great time doing it, too. After the music was done, they all took their bow and pranced off the stage.

When I think about these precious little girls, I realize that when God looks at me, that's what He sees. He sees the things that we call imperfections and defines them as beauty. He looks on us with joy as we go through life not always knowing which way to turn, feeling as if we look like a fool to everyone else around us. He delights in you and in me just the way we are. We are His children and He loves us, no matter what we do wrong or how stupid we might think we look. It brings Him great joy to watch us grow up and become more like Him.

Jesus was perfect. He lived this life completely as a man and never sinned. He never once gave into temptation from the enemy. That doesn't necessarily mean He didn't trip and fall, does it? Do you think that He always hit the right pitch when He sang? I honestly don't know the answer to that because I wasn't there, but I'm pretty sure His feet got dirty when He was walking the desert roads. I'm confident that Jesus had fun when He walked the earth as a man, and He probably was a whole lot of fun to be around.

I'm not sure if He would laugh at his disciples if they fell out of the boat while they were fishing (I know I would have), but I honestly think that He just might have shared a few laughs with them. Again, I don't know for sure on that, but for Jesus to be God's son, He must have a great sense of humor and lots of joy and life in Him as He walked the earth.

Perfection Defined

Our definition of perfection in our society is way off base. We look at all of what we consider failures and define them as imperfections. We look at the fact that our house isn't clean and that the laundry isn't put away, and we allow that to get us down and make us think less of ourselves. Then comes the stress. Why?

The definition of the word perfect as found on Dictionary.com is as follows:

Perfect: conforming absolutely to the description or definition of an ideal type.[6]

This definition hit me in so many ways. First of all, let me just share with you how amazing our God is. When we gave our lives to Christ we became perfect. I know this may be difficult for many to understand, but in Hebrews 10:14 it says this: but by one sacrifice he has made perfect forever those who are being made holy.

When we surrendered our lives to Christ we immediately became perfect. That means when God sees us, He sees absolute perfection. We now, because of Christ, conform absolutely (just like the definition above) to the description of the ideal type of God, just like Adam and Eve did before they sinned. We no longer have sin that separates us. We have been forgiven and made perfect. Period. We don't have to strive for perfection to please God because we've already been made perfect. Our actions have no bearing whatsoever on the way God sees us. We're forgiven because of Jesus and we've been made perfect. Perfection is in us, and it actually *defines* who we are.

That's it. I'm not saying that we don't sin anymore, but all of our sins have been washed away. We now are living out our holiness. If we know Jesus, we conform to God's ideal. Jesus did that for us! How amazing is that! We can fellowship with Him, love Him, hear his voice and walk with Him, just as Adam and Eve did. We can have a close relationship with the Creator of the world, our Maker and Father, because of Jesus!

Are You Critical?

Being critical of other people has become an openly accepted part of our culture these days. Why is it that I'm drawn to watch a show like American Idol and sit there critiquing all of the singers? Why do I think that I have the ear for the perfect song or singer and that they should sing according to the way I think they should? Why do the judges have the right to criticize? Don't get me wrong, I'll sit there with the best of them and join right in. It doesn't matter what the person might have gone through that day; if they stink, then they should go home. How did they make it that far anyway?

We all have adapted a sense of what we consider to be perfect, based on what goes on around us. We've created this ideal that a singer is considered perfect if they hit the pitch just right, not being sharp or flat. I know when I was studying the different types of music from around the world, perfect pitch wasn't even considered. It was difficult for me to even listen to some of the chants and ways of singing from other regions of the world because it wasn't "perfect" to me. Why do we always think our way is better? I guess because that's what we were taught. That's how we grew up, and so we tend to place all of these "perfect" expectations on others that aren't even from God. We expect others to live the same way we do, and if they don't, they're not doing it "right." We'll gossip about them and think less of them simply because God made them differently.

I'm not saying that if someone is living in sin that it's okay. Of course that's not the case. Even if that were the case, we still don't have room to be critical. But if someone simply keeps their house a little messier than we do, we shouldn't be critical. If someone dresses differently, talks with a different accent, or looks unlike us, it shouldn't matter. Their definition of "perfection" is not the same. If someone's way of living is blatantly against the Word of God, then we have a right to say something in love, of course; otherwise, we probably should keep our opinions to ourselves unless we're asked.

I'm definitely guilty of doing this, especially at home. My husband seems to have a different taste in clothing than I do—in particularly when it comes to cowboy boots. We've been married now for 15 years and he finally got these boots that he's been wanting for so long. I've never once in my life desired such a thing, so I would always try to talk him out of it, but finally he got a pair for his birthday last year. Not only did he get them, my 6 year old son got some and absolutely loves them! He wears them with his shorts or sweatpants or whatever he's wearing. It doesn't matter because he loves his boots!

My definition of what looks good isn't necessarily the same as my husband Chris' or even now, my son Stephen's, or for that matter, the rest of the world. I shouldn't complain when they choose what they want to wear and should not be so overbearing in my opinions, because that's just what they are—opinions. I really shouldn't give my thoughts on the matter at all, unless I'm asked or feel like what he's wearing might jeopardize something important (i.e. a job interview). If he wants to wear cowboy boots with sweat shorts he has every right to do so. I don't need to be critical. My way is not always right.

Self Imposed Perfection

Perfectionism can be very precarious. Many times we set up an ideal for our lives that doesn't even come from God. We think it's from God because it's something good, but it's really an expectation we come up with ourselves that isn't based on God or His Word at all. In fact many of the things we do are instigated by the enemy. We expect ourselves to meet certain goals or ideals that are simply unreasonable. Our attempt to attain these goals or the type of lifestyle we think we want may keep us from God and deepening our relationship with Him as well as the people He's placed in our lives. Not to mention it makes us feel like a failure if we don't accomplish these goals or ideals.

The bottom line is that God is deeply in love with each one of us, and He desires an intimate relationship with us. Some will give their lives to Christ and hardly ever speak to Him after that. Sure they might go to church every Sunday, but that has no bearing on how they are relating with God. They might call on Him during a hard time or even say a prayer for their friend's mom who has cancer, but that's it. There is no consistent fellowship between them and God. Having a short devotion every morning is a great thing, but God wants every part of our day. He wants us to fellowship with Him everywhere we go and in everything we do.

Take Mary and Martha for example. In Luke 10:38-42 the story is told of two sisters, Mary and Martha who are both friends with Jesus. As you probably remember, Jesus visits them and Mary is distracted by all the preparations. Martha complains to Jesus because

Mary isn't helping her with any of them and Jesus simply replies, "Martha, Martha, you are worried and upset about many things, but only one thing is needed. Mary has chosen what is better, and it will not be taken away from her."

I imagine Martha was a perfectionist. She wanted everything to look and be just right for Jesus. However Jesus said only one thing is needed. Only one thing, and that *is* Jesus. It's not all the preparations we make. It's not having our house perfect for company. It's not getting rid of all the germs or appearing perfect on the outside. It's not what everyone else thinks, or impressing those around us. It's not getting our kids from the soccer game to dance class on time. It's not getting the new car or even having someone like you. It's not being debt-free or living in a big house. It's not even serving Jesus at church, leading a Bible study, or moving to Africa to be a missionary. The one thing is Jesus. Nothing else is needed. Nothing. Nothing compares to being in constant fellowship with Him in this life, and nothing comes close to the importance of allowing Him to love you and the importance of you loving Him.

Everything we do should be authored by Him. It's not good to do something just because we feel like we should. Martha didn't have to make those preparations. Jesus didn't need that. He just wanted her heart.

So many serve their hearts out, just like Martha did. They come to church all the time, run the kids ministry, run the welcome table, and lead a small group. The problem with this is, in many cases, their actual relationship with Jesus is almost non-existent. Chris and I used to do college campus ministry, and we had hosted a numerous amount of cookouts for the students. Chris would always be the one to be cooking at the grill. As he liked to put it in later years, he'd "hide behind the grill." This would keep him from having to interact with anyone. It made him appear to be a great servant, but really he was running from any kind of interaction with others.

So many of us are "hiding behind the grill" or hiding behind running the small group or some other ministry. I know many people who hide behind their work of any kind. To these types of people, doing work or serving always takes first priority over just hanging out and fellowshipping with others. We should always check our motives before we serve in any capacity in life. Jesus said that one thing is necessary, and that is fellowship with Him. Chances are if we're "hiding behind the grill," we're also hiding from God. If we're too busy doing everything else, our priorities are definitely mixed up.

This includes churches as well as individuals. There are always so many programs and so many events for non-Christians. We all get so busy running these events that we forget why we're doing them in the first place. If we'd spend our time in communion with the lover of our souls, passionately sitting at his feet and building our relationship with Him, all else would fall into place. He is the priority. He's the one thing. He's what makes life perfect.

Some might feel like God will love them less if they don't go to church every time the doors are open. Consequently, others might feel like God will love them more if they do go to church every time the doors are open. This is a type of perfectionism that is based solely on deeds.

God simply wants us to be who He has made us to be. In Matthew 5, Jesus talks about this very plainly. He's describing all the different laws of the past and how as we follow God, we will actually surpass these ways of living. He shows us that not only do we need to not commit adultery, but that if someone looks lustfully at another person that it's just as bad as adultery. He says that it was written to "love your neighbor and hate your enemy," but we're to take it a step further and love our enemies and even pray for those who persecute us. In verse 48 Jesus goes on to say the following: "Be perfect, therefore, as your heavenly Father is perfect."

You might ask, well how in the world can we do that? Remember what we talked about earlier? Jesus has come and set us free from the chains of the law, and because of His sacrifice, we already ARE perfect if He is the Lord of our lives. If we've repented and made Him the king, then we've been made perfect, just like Jesus was saying here. Sometimes I want to jump up and shout when I hear that!

He is showing us that we need not set up all these rules and regulations for our lives that establish a false sense of perfection. We should be perfect like our heavenly Father is perfect, to live the life set out before us that God has called us to, not putting all of these weighty restrictions and rules on ourselves. That is so freeing! To know that I'm loved and accepted by God just the way I am, faults and all, is such an amazing revelation. God wants us to be free to love Him without restraint!

Placing My Perfect Rules on Others

The gift of a real friend is such a blessing, and God really has poured out His blessing on me through the years with amazing friends. I have learned, however, that I have had a tendency to place my "rules of perfect friendship" on my close friends. I thought that I knew best when it came to relationships, so if my friends didn't act the way that I thought they should, something was wrong with them.

God has definitely taught me this principle the hard way. When a friend comes into my life that I want to get to know better, I'll usually go out of my way to make time for them, and I will even give them cards every now and then or even little gifts to show the person that I care and value our relationship. While all of these are nice gestures, it's been my tendency to place an unspoken rule on the other person to do something in return: a thank you note with their deep gratitude or a phone call saying how much it meant to them that I had done this "selfless" act of generosity. Unfortunately that's not how it always worked. In most cases, the gesture was genuinely appreciated and received in such a way that showed me the feeling was mutual, but it definitely didn't always happen that way...and it shouldn't have.

On a couple of different occasions with friends I have been challenged on this very issue. They thought I was trying to change them into something that they weren't. If they didn't respond like I felt they should, I would get hurt and communicate my hurt feelings to them, when it wasn't their fault at all. It was my definition of a "perfect" friendship that was the problem. I had to do a deep soul searching to find out that I was indeed trying to make them the type of friend that I am, instead of the type friend God had made them to be. I was expecting something from them that they never desired to give or that weren't ready to give, holding it against them because they didn't do it the "perfect" way that I had deemed a friend should.

Just because I felt a deep connection with that friend and wanted to show it by writing a card or some other gesture didn't mean that they felt the same way in return, and they didn't need to. I had created this "ideal friend" that nobody could ever live up to. Thankfully these friends chose to see through that and continue to stick with me. I have been so blessed by the friends that God has given to me, despite my incorrect expectations.

When we think of young kids, they seem to live out this type of life everyday. They don't worry what others think. They don't care what they look like. They seem to know that they are perfect just the way they are. They have patience with themselves and don't expect too much of themselves or others. They go through life with a smile because they haven't yet been inundated with the ways of the world. They don't know yet that they should color within the lines. They just color the way they want. Grass doesn't always have to be green. Skies are really pretty when they're purple or orange or even black.

What's great, though, when a child colors a picture it goes on the fridge. Just like when we live life for God. God always puts our "imperfect" pictures on display for all to see. We are perfectly imperfect. What a great God of love we serve. I'm so thankful that He sees me as perfect just the way I am!

Part 2

Free to Jump!

I DO know everything, just not THAT!
–Stephen Sharpe, age 4

I told my PreK students, "There are many types of nuts: peanuts, hazelnuts, walnuts... What is your favorite?" One replied, "My favorite nut is a doughnut." (<u>Heardontheplayground.com</u>)

As I was putting on my "favorite" pair of jeans, you know the one you can't get rid of because it makes you feel and look skinny...well I lied down on my bed with the door shut, sucking in my gut getting blisters as I was pulling up my zipper. At that very moment, my son walks in and says sweetly, "Mommy, do you need help pushing in your fat?" (<u>Heardontheplayground.com</u>)

Chapter 4

Free to Dream Big

"Mommy, will I buy my own clothes when I grow up?"
"Of course you will, Hope!" "Well, what will I wear to go get
them?" - Hope Sharpe, age 5

I've often contemplated of dreams and ambitions during my life, wondering if they will ever come to pass. Watching children and talking to them about their dreams and what they want to be when they grow up truly amazes me. They are not afraid to dream big, to think big, to wonder about what they're going to be one day or what they are going to accomplish in the future. They don't have any fear about that at all.

When I think about my kids and the way they believe, it makes me realize how much they have inside to accomplish in this life. My oldest wants to dance, sing, draw, and she's also doing well at school. One of her main dreams is to be a beautician. She is so young yet is so amazing at doing hair! I can't even braid someone's hair, but she, at the age of 9 can do just about any style you can imagine. She wants so much to be great and to fulfill her dreams, and what's even better is that she realizes she IS great! It seems that kids only stop believing that can accomplish their dreams when an adult who "knows better" tells them something different.

Dreaming can be so much fun! It's great to think about the future and dream about what might be in store for you. Will I be married? I wonder what my husband will be like. I wonder if I'll have kids or a great career. I wonder. There are so many things to look forward to in life. The great thing is that we can still dream even if we're over 40…or 60…or even 90!

Dreaming Despite the Odds

I was driving past a billboard a while ago, and I saw a great advertisement about perseverance. It featured a woman at the age of 95, and she had just become the oldest college graduate. She had fulfilled one of her dreams. How great! It encouraged to me to see someone her age realize that she is not simply on the earth to take up space, but to pursue what she desires in her heart.

This is what's so great about kids. They dare to dream. They're not afraid to want to be president or even the next Michael Jordan. Who are we to tell them they can't? Who are we to tell ourselves or our adult friends that *we* can't? I believe that we live life much too conservatively. We don't take chances, and we're afraid to let what's inside of us come out. That needs to change. We need to be careful not to let the world around us or our fears define what God strategically placed inside of us. People think that they are doing us a favor by telling us *their* opinions about *our* dreams. All of these different voices may make us afraid to go after the desires that God has placed inside of us.

In the movie "Morning Glory," there is a scene where a mother is talking to her 28 year old daughter whose life-long dream is to be the next executive producer of the "Today" show on NBC. Her whole life revolves around this dream, and she is really good at what she does. When she gets fired at her local news job, she begins looking for another job, and her mother tells her this:

> *"You think the Today show is going to call you up and offer you a job? This is partly my fault. I let your father get your hopes up. You had a dream, you know, great! When you were 8 it was adorable. When you were eighteen it was inspiring. At 28, it's officially embarrassing. And I just want you to stop before we get to heartbreaking."[7]*

It's almost as if we feel it's childish to still believe…to still hope…and to continue to have faith that there is more to this life than just the daily grind. We settle in to a job that is just okay. We've lost our hope, believing it to be impossible to live life this way. We tend to look down on those people who step out of the box and jump. We get jealous of the people who, like Peter, decide to step out of the boat and trust Jesus while they're doing the impossible. *We are called to do the impossible!* Jesus called us to believe like children believe. Jesus called us to do greater things ON THIS EARTH than He did while He walked these roads himself (John 14:12). **We are not only called to be great. We *are* great.**

It's interesting to me that when we are children we believe in what we can become. We know that nothing is impossible. Even other people believed in us as they cheered us on. We heard, "You can do it! Good job. You can be whatever you want to be when you grow up, if you just believe in yourself." Why all of a sudden when we get older do people start telling us that we *can't* do it? Why do people say that we're never going to fulfill the dreams that God has placed in our hearts? I think there are a couple of reasons for this, and it produces some results that are not from God.

Opposition from Others

I've come to the conclusion that others stop believing in us when we become older because many times they are bitter inside. They have perhaps realized that *they* haven't been running their race with excellence, so they don't want anyone else to either. If they're not going to be successful in life, they surely don't want you to be because that means that you are "better" than they are.

The truth is that these types of people are hurting, and they also need to know that they also have a divine destiny. I don't know if you've ever felt this way, but there have been many times in my life where I secretly didn't want someone to succeed due to my own failures and shortcomings. Instead of cheering that person on and being encouraged by their success, I would get bitter and jealous. My heart would get hurt because their accomplishments made me feel like more of a failure. I secretly wanted to be the one to succeed first.

The second reason I think people give up on others is because they don't believe the TRUTH to be true anymore. People get caught up in the way the world is doing things, blinded by fear and negativity, and they stop believing life can be fulfilling and that you *can* live a life filled joy and success, despite the circumstances. It's become the norm in our society to be busy and stressed out, on the go all the time, and never satisfied. That does not sound like the promises of God to me. God says that we will have life in abundance, full of peace and joy, if we live life in step with Him and the direction of the Holy Spirit.

That doesn't mean trials won't come our way, it's just that we are prepared when they come because we know that God WILL take care of us. God never breaks his promises, it's just that *we* don't seem to fully trust Him to do what He said. If people don't believe that what God says is going to happen, then why would they ever encourage *you* to believe it? Why would they ever encourage you to pursue your dreams if they don't believe that it is possible to achieve them?

We have dreams, and they were put inside our hearts for a reason. God made us who we are so we can fulfill those dreams that He placed inside of us. There is not another person on this earth called to be you. You are the only one. Sure, some dreams may not come to pass immediately, or maybe they won't ever come to pass while we're still on this earth, but when they are God-given dreams that He's placed in your heart, for us not to believe we can do it is the same as telling God that He can't do it. After all, He's the one who made us. He made us in His image. His son died for us and now lives in us (if, of course, you've surrendered your life to Him), and because He lives in us, nothing at all is impossible with God (Luke 1:37). Absolutely nothing.

Nothing is Impossible

Just reminisce for a moment with me on some very amazing people that God moved through in history. Think about Abraham. A man who was almost 100 years old, and his wife was 90. He was childless, yet

God named him the father of many nations. Childless at 100. Impossible for God? Nope. He became the father of many nations, just as it was said of him. Why? Because he believed. Take the prostitute, Rahab. She was definitely not someone who was a role model for us...except when she chose to believe God. She spared the lives of the men of God and because of this, her whole household was spared and she was in the lineage of Jesus. Yes, Jesus, the King of all kings and Savior of the world was a direct descendant of the prostitute, Rahab. She chose to believe and honor God, and in turn, she was honored by God.

What about Daniel? He was thrown in the Lion's den because of he refused to bow down to anyone but God. Did he get eaten? Nope. He believed God, trusting that nothing was impossible, and he knew that God would spare his life supernaturally. He chose to believe that God was bigger than what he was facing.

How about David? He's one of my favorites. David, a young shepherd, was looked down upon by his brothers. He didn't even go out to war with them when Goliath, the Philistine, came and threatened Israel.

When David went to deliver some food to his brothers, he asked this simple question, "Who is this uncircumcised Philistine that He should defy the armies of the living God?" David clearly knew his position, and He knew that absolutely nothing was impossible for him through the power of God. He was a young boy facing about a 9-10 foot tall man. He went out in the power of God with faith and with one simple stone, he defeated the giant.

One stone is all it took. I believe that one step is all it takes for us. One step towards all that God has for us. One step in choosing to believe Him for great things in our lives. One step to turn away from being afraid of the things and the ways of thinking that hold us back from God's absolute best for us. One step. Then another. Then another. Knowing that God is with you all the way. Knowing that the impossible is within your grasp because the One who formed the universe lives inside of you.

Do you get it? The ONE who formed the universe is IN YOU! The same Spirit that raised Christ from the dead is living in you!(Rom. 8:11) Are you living a dead life? Are you living a mundane life that isn't going anywhere or making any kind of difference? You have a choice. Will you choose to believe God and what He says as a child believes, or will you believe what you've been told all your life? Will you worry about what everyone else thinks, or will you be concerned with pleasing the One who is passionate about you and longs to see your dreams come to pass even more than you do?

Laurin's Story

There was a time in my life when I desperately wanted to have children. Before this particular time in my life, I didn't have a strong desire to have any kids, but all of a sudden that desire appeared from nowhere, and after two years of marriage, I felt it was time to begin our family.

Little did I know that my monthly cycle was not happening the way it should be. I had a false sense that everything was working properly when I was taking the birth control pills, and as soon as I stopped, so did my monthly cycle. It makes it difficult to have kids without that! I visited the doctor, and the first thing he did was put me on some medicine to get it started again—and that's just what happened. The only problem was that my cycle wasn't working unless I was taking the medicine.

About a year into this, the doctor decided it was time to put me on the first round of fertility medicine. I took the first prescription to get my cycle started, and then, when that happened, I took the fertility meds.

My emotions were all over the place during this. It was hard to continually believe God that my dream of having children would come to pass because things in my body weren't working right. I'd cry out to Him every single day, asking Him to fulfill this dream that I believed He'd placed in my heart.

God and I would go on long walks together. I'd always bring my note cards with scripture verses on them and build myself up, knowing that this was something that God wanted for us. Every month when the time came, I'd hold my breath and get out yet another pregnancy test. I was always afraid to look at it, but when I finally mustered up the courage to flip it over, it would be negative.

Time and time again I had "one-liners," and time and time again it would break my heart. I'd run back to God in tears, wondering what in the world was wrong with me. Why was this so hard? Everyone else around me was getting pregnant. Why in the world couldn't I?

During this time the Lord encouraged my heart. One day in particular I remember going for my walk, and again I had my scripture cards with me. As I was flipping through them, I came across Psalm 37:4 – a verse that I had read many times before, except this day it took on a whole new meaning.

It says this: "Delight yourself in the Lord and He will give you the desires of your heart." Up until this point I had been consumed with praying for a baby. Every time I'd go to the Lord, having a child was the first, middle, and last thing that I'd pray for. I wanted it so badly that I would have done just about anything. God was showing me that it was not about the promise or the dream, but about the One who gave it to me. Without Him, there would be no dream. I was delighting myself in the idea of having a child, rather than being satisfied with Him and delighting in His presence.

At that point I surrendered this dream of having a baby to Him, and He encouraged my heart. I let it go, placing it in His hands, knowing that His will is best. It was not easy, but I came to the point in my heart that my relationship with God was more valuable than anything He could give to me. I told Him that I'd be satisfied with Him, even if nothing ever happened. Of course my heart was screaming this whole time, but I knew that everything would be okay.

It's common knowledge that when you're attempting to get pregnant you can take your temperature every morning when you wake up to determine what part of your monthly cycle you are in. I would do this just about every morning to see if my body was working properly, and with the pills, it definitely was. That gave me hope.

One evening when we were visiting my parents I felt God speak to my heart and ask me to stop taking the medicine. I was not convinced at first that this was the Lord because I knew that things were finally working properly and looking up. So I decided to "fleece."

If you read in the book of Judges, the Lord spoke to Gideon, but to make sure it was really a word from God, Gideon decided to place a fleece out on the ground. He then asked the Lord to make the fleece wet with dew in the morning, but the ground would be dry. God agreed, and that's exactly what happened. The next night Gideon, still not convinced it was God, did the same thing again. This time it was reversed. He asked that the ground be wet and that the fleece be dry.[8]   It was. God was confirming His Word to Gideon through this act.

I decided to fleece about this decision that was about to take place. It was something I felt released to do by God, so I knew that it was okay to ask God to do this. I said to the Lord, "God, if my temperature is 98.5 tomorrow morning when I wake up, I will stop taking the medicine." It wasn't time for my temperature to go up, but I asked anyway. I told Chris about it before we went to bed that night, and he was anxiously waiting to find out what would happen just like I was.

So, that faithful July morning came and the first thing I did was grab the thermometer. I don't even remember if I prayed or not, but I quickly turned it on, put it in my mouth and waited. When the sound went off and it was done, I looked down and my temperature was exactly what I had asked for it to be. 98.5. I couldn't believe it! That day I chose to quit taking my medicine and believe God.

September 29, 2001 I took another pregnancy test. It was not a one-liner this time. Just two months after obeying God, my dreams had finally come to pass. Nine months after that day I was holding a beautiful baby girl in my arms. And now God has blessed us with three amazing kids, and a surprise blessing on the way. God is faithful.

The Kingdom of God Defined

I believe that doing what God calls you to do is identical to bringing the kingdom of God here on this earth. In the Amplified Bible the kingdom of God is defined as "God's way of doing things." If God's way of doing things for your life is to become what He's placed on your heart, then as you are obedient and fulfill His desires for your life, you're bringing the Kingdom of God more and more into your life.

If you "seek first His kingdom" (Matt. 6:33), then all these things will be added to you as well. If you do what God calls you to do, then everything else will fall into place. That doesn't mean there won't be opposition. In fact, when you step out and obey God, even more opposition arises. If you're sitting around waiting for your dreams to come to you, chances are you won't find much opposition because you're not moving anywhere.

If you're called to the mission field and you obey God, He will provide all of your needs. You might have to work hard to raise your support, but God's grace will be in it. It won't just fall in your lap. If God is calling you to start your own company, He will make a way if you just step out. But you must step out. Faith without action is dead (James 2:20). He will provide if you just believe. It will be done according to your faith.[9] It's about believing, stepping out, and knowing that the impossible is within your grasp because of Jesus. If your dreams aren't way bigger than you, then chances are they are not God's dreams for your life. If your dreams are all about you and not His kingdom, then they're also not God's best for you.

Many times we get so stuck in the rut of everyday life that we've lost sight of having any dreams at all. If this is where you are, I want to encourage you to ask God to show you what He wants to accomplish in you and through you. Ask God to drop a new dream into your heart. I guarantee if you ask, God will answer. Many of us probably don't even want to ask God because when He shows us something, we then become responsible to follow through with it, which requires a faith that's beyond ourselves. Dreaming big isn't easy, and stepping out to live that dream can be even more challenging, but God will always be there to empower you to do way more than you could do on your own.

The Bible in Proverbs 29:18 (KJV) says, "Where there is no vision, the people perish." If there is no vision for your life, or if you don't have a dream that you are going after, you might want to do a serious check on your inner-life and your dreams. If you don't have vision for your life, you're perishing. You're headed nowhere, and the days are quickly passing by. Time is running out!

I've watched it time and time again when people reach retirement age. Everyone is so excited to retire and start taking life easy for a change. I'm definitely not putting down retirement, but in many cases after people quit their jobs they lose their vision. They don't have anything to aim for anymore, so they begin to perish.

It's amazing how quickly someone ages when they have no goals in life. Even in my life when I don't know where I'm going, I begin to feel hopeless and depressed.

My heart in life is to do what I'm called to do. To finish the race that is set before me and when I reach the end of my days to hear those words we, as sons and daughters of God, long to hear: "Well done, good and faithful servant."[10] When we wander aimlessly, we become like the Israelites in the desert. They had a place to go, but it took 40 years to get them to the Promised Land because of their disobedience and fear. We, as children of God, have a divine purpose in this life. Pleasing Him, being in relationship with Him, and telling others about Him is our purpose.

So remember to "expect great things from God and attempt great things for God." William Carey said it best. Nothing is impossible with God. No dream is too big to attain...only believe...just like a child would, and watch God move in greater ways than you can fathom.

My five-year-old daughter is an aspiring firefighter. Yesterday, as she was thumbing through a book on firefighting, she saw a picture of a "fire dog" (a Dalmatian). She looked at me seriously and said, "You never see fire cats. If there was a fire, they'd just lie around."

My daughter was in Kindergarten and she had a boy try to kiss her. I was discussing this with her and I asked her if she had kissed any boys she said "No mom, you don't see a ring on this finger do you?"

SUSAN (age 4) was drinking juice when she got the hiccups. "Please don't give me this juice again," she said, "It makes my teeth cough."
(www.HeardonthePlayground.com)

Chapter 5

Free to Completely Trust

My three-year old was telling my two-year old that Jesus has everything in His hands. She said, "The sun, the stars, the moon, everything!" Then she added, "I hope He's careful with the sun, though, it gets really hot!

"Okay, Laurin, jump to me! It's okay; I promise I will catch you!"

How many times have we seen parents with their children at the pool trying to persuade their kid to jump off the edge into their arms? I know I did it just about every time I went to the pool with my kids—at least until they decided they could jump in on their own. Most of the time they were afraid when I'd ask them to jump, saying to me, "Okay, I'll jump, but let me hold your hands." Or they would say, "Mommy, are you SURE you will catch me? I'm afraid!"

It's not something that they loved to do, at least not at first. I suppose they were petrified that mommy or daddy wouldn't catch them and that they'd end up at the bottom of the pool. Eventually, after they jumped enough times, they quickly understood that there was nothing to be afraid of and that yes, mommy actually WILL catch them. After they figured this out, they never wanted to STOP jumping in, and mommy got very tired!

Trust is a big issue. Trusting God completely is not something that many people do in life today. Jumping into a deep pool when He says "Jump!" can be daunting. Many of us trust Him with certain things but not with others. Most of us trust God when the circumstances are going great in our lives and when the checkbook says we're doing well, but when the times get tough and circumstances aren't so good, we tend to turn our back on God. We forget that He is trustworthy and that He will never fail us.

My Difficulties in Trusting God

I would have to say that my biggest trust issue in life has been in dealing with finances. Before I got married and had kids, finances were no big deal. I always had what I needed. My dad had a very secure job and finances seemed easy. They seemed to budget money well, and they were always faithful to give. Even when I was in college, I never had to work. I got a full scholarship and whatever other expenses that arose, my parents would be right there to help.

When I got married, things changed. We had no debt and both of us had jobs and a place to live that was within our budget. Then came the time where we made a few unwise decisions. We made a rather large purchase and decided to put it on a credit card, and thus began a downward spiral into debt. Shortly after that purchase, we felt like God was calling us into full-time ministry. With that decision we had to raise financial support for our salary, which in itself was a major challenge and test of faith.

I was always thankful for our partners' generosity; however, we never had a very consistent paycheck. When we did have a consistent paycheck, it was not enough to meet the needs of our growing family. I would worry month after month, wondering if we were going to make enough to pay the bills. This would cause so much tension between Chris and me, and many times I found myself extremely angry because I felt like this wasn't the life I was expecting when we got married. I never saw my parents go through any of these difficulties, and I never ever expected my marriage to be any different. I had an expectation that the man needed to be the "bread winner," and in my heart I was very hurt and disappointed with Chris. I didn't feel like I could trust him to take care of me the way I thought I needed to be taken care of.

I also felt as if I couldn't trust God, either. After all, He called us into ministry. Why did it seem like He wasn't providing? Why were we short so often, and why were we under so much stress? The way that I felt towards Chris and God was my choice, just to clarify. I felt like I needed someone to blame, and they were the most obvious ones, so I started feeling resentment towards both of them — though neither of them had done anything wrong.

It came to a point, even with my three small children, where I felt like I needed to do something about it. I knew in my heart that God had called me to do ministry and to be a stay at home mother, but since the needs weren't being met the way *I thought they should be*, I decided to start looking for a job.

I found a job working at Kid's Club at Gold's gym. This was the first job I had after having kids besides working in ministry. It was fine, but I barely got paid anything for the hours and the time I put into it. I would drag my kids with me everyday, but it quickly became tiring. It definitely wasn't God's best for our family. About six months into it, I decided to quit and try to find something better.

Time and time again I would do the same thing. Job after job, I dragged the kids with me trying to make ends meet, because I felt like God and my husband weren't getting the job done, and the debt just kept growing and growing. At one point I was working three different jobs and trying to be a successful wife and mom. I dragged the kids with me while doing deliveries of free publications, I had an at home data entry job, and I was working part-time in the office at my church. It stressed me out beyond belief, and I could never focus on any one thing because something else was always hanging over my head.

All of these things were not because I felt called to do them, but because I wasn't trusting God to provide. Every time I got a job I never felt at peace. It's not like these jobs were bad, they just weren't God's best for me. I was making decisions because of my lack of trust, based solely on our financial situation...not on God's word.

The Love of Money

I'm sure you've heard the scripture in 1 Timothy 6:10 that states "The love of money is the root of all evil." I've always imagined that verse to be pertaining to people who are well-off, flaunting their money and possessions for everyone to look at. While I'm sure it includes them as well, God showed me that in my pursuit of all of these different things, the decision to make money at all costs came well above His plan for my life and my trust that He would meet my needs.

People without a lot of wealth can love money just as much as the wealthy can—they just don't have it at their disposal. Their pursuit of wealth at all costs, or even the pursuit of "just making ends meet" is just as detrimental to following Jesus as flaunting what you have to impress others. Our pursuit is Jesus, not money or anything else. Our trust is in God, not in a job or any other mission.

With all of this in mind, I finally chose to follow Christ and give up my last job. Since then I had a long season where I didn't work at all. Now, God has provided a job where I can stay at home and watch two of my friends' children, and I have much more free time to be able to do the things that God has called me to do. Sure, when things get tight financially, I start wondering if I'm doing the right thing. God then confirms that I am on His path, giving me amazing amounts of peace in my life. He's showing me that I don't need to run after another job to make ends meet, since He has called us to be full-time ministers. He will provide much better for us than any job ever could. Of course, if I'm feeling led by the Spirit to go out and get an additional job, then I would need to trust God to bring me to the right one, and He would.

When I start feeling unsure about our finances and I feel anxious, I turn to the Word of God. I remind myself that Proverbs 10:22 says that "The blessing of the Lord brings wealth, and he adds no trouble to it." Toiling and doing everything in my power to make ends meet does not bring any more of God's blessing. In fact it has the opposite effect. There are promises in the Bible that God wants us to hold in our hearts so when times get tough and our trust is failing we can hold onto His Word.

I came to realize that I was allowing our financial situation and my lack of trust in God define who I was.

My actions were displaying a belief that I couldn't do what God had called me to do because of my finances. That was simply untrue. God promises to restore all things. If He can die on the cross to save the sins of the world, surely He's big enough to pay my bills. You might think to yourself, "Well, I got myself into this debt. It's not God's fault. It's my responsibility to get myself out." Well, with that kind of thinking, what about sin? Aren't you the one who chose to sin and go against God? Didn't He forgive you for that? It's all about His work in our lives, not ours. It's about accepting His free gift to us, obeying Him, and letting go of our old lifestyle.

How do I Become Free to Trust?

I guess all of this leads me to the great question: How do you become free to trust completely, like a child does? How do you walk though life with peace in your heart, knowing that God will take care of all of your greatest (and not so great) needs? How do we know this to be true and live by it everyday?

If you look at a 3-year old, that child has no concern whatsoever for his life. Jesus even says in Matthew to look at the lilies of the field and the birds of the air and how He has clothed them. He goes on to say "how much more will He take care of you?"[11] Jesus says in Matthew 6:33 to "Seek first the kingdom of God, and all these things will be added unto you." So, how does this get down into your heart? How do you trust God to take care of your children when you send them off to school everyday? How do you trust God to provide financially when you know that what comes in isn't enough to pay the bills every month? How do you trust God to repair your marriage when you haven't felt in love with your spouse in years? How do you trust God to bring you peace when everything around you is screaming otherwise?

Just look at a 3-year old. They don't know where their next meal is coming from, yet they trust mommy or daddy to provide it for them. God is the same way, except much better. He is faithful to keep all of His promises.

So how do you trust Him completely to take care of you in every single area of your life? The answer is this: you get to know Him. You read His amazing word, filled with all His incredible promises. You spend time with Him, telling Him of your fears, pouring your heart out to Him and letting Him bring you peace. You take steps of faith in certain areas you know God is calling you to, even when your old self would be screaming, NO! You do things even if you're afraid, and watch God move. You choose to jump off the edge into His arms because HE says He will catch you. You obey Him at all costs. He promises to never leave you or forsake you. He promises to meet your every need. He promises to answer you when you call. And He is completely faithful to all of these promises.

The more you get to know God, the more you will trust Him. The more you stop depending on yourself to take care of everything, the more you start depending on the Creator — the One who is passionately in love with you who would never want you to come to ruin.

The Bible promises that He will never let the righteous fall, and you'll never see them begging for bread.[12] Guess what? If you know Jesus and have been forgiven, YOU ARE RIGHTEOUS! You go through the Bible and read stories like I mentioned in the previous chapter of how God saved Daniel from the Lion's den, how He defeated the Egyptians, how He made the Red

Sea part, how God brought people back to life, how He defeated entire countries with just a few people, and you realize that your little problem is nothing compared to what God can and WILL do for you.

He is utterly trustworthy and faithful. He never ever fails on His promises...EVER. He will take care of your family, your children, your health, and YOU. He loves you and wants to see you succeed in life even more than you do. He is for you, not against you (Romans 8:31), and He has an amazing plan in store for your life. Just get to know Him. Fall in love with Him. Trust Him. Follow Him. Lay down your life for Him and you will be totally blown away by what God will do for you. You can never spend too much time with God; there will always be more to learn about Him.

That's why it's so important to spend time with God and in the Bible everyday. It's vitally important to memorize scripture—not just so you can have something nice to quote every now and then, but because it's a tool to use when you feel yourself starting to doubt God.

If you know that God is your provider, then when the devil comes at you saying you're going to go bankrupt because you don't have enough money, you immediately know that that thought is against God, so it can't be true. If the enemy comes to you trying to convince you that you're going to get cancer because it runs in your family, that is not a promise from God! It's something that comes straight from the enemy and he's trying to get you to not trust the Word. If you know that God says in His Word that you are healed and whole, then you can immediately come against what the devil is saying and put your trust in what God is saying.

Knowing God, His character, and the truth of His Word gives you the strength to be able to stand against the devil and unbelief. It gives you the strength to trust

Him at His Word. When you get to know someone, you trust them a whole lot more. When you go deeper with Jesus, you know that He has great plans for you and you know that He never fails on His promises, even when the devil is trying to convince you otherwise.

One very important thing to remember through your journey of trust, however, is that many times the way we feel things should happen, isn't necessarily the way they always play out. We want our healing, finances, family members' salvation or whatever else immediately, when that's not always the way God chooses to fulfill these promises.

Yes, all of these are still His Word and many times when they don't get fulfilled the way we think they should, we give up and stop believing. We don't believe in our hearts that He will do what He says. That's the moment when real faith kicks in – that moment when we don't feel it in our hearts, but choose to continue to believe in His faithfulness despite what's going on around us. His promises are fulfilled on His time and in His way, not ours...but they are fulfilled, indeed.

So, when you're feeling down and afraid, remember that the God you serve is a trustworthy, faithful God who will never let you down. He might not do everything the way you think He should, because His way is so much better. He might not give you what you think you need, but trust Him...He's got something so much better in store. Your plan for your life cannot even come close to the great plan that God has for you, if you'll just trust Him and...JUMP!

STEVEN (age 3) hugged and kissed his Mom good night. "I love you so much that when you die I'm going to bury you outside my bedroom window." (Heardontheplayground.com)

During a conversation about communion at church, one of the girls said, "They ought to make vanilla-flavored wafer," To which another girl replied, "Yeah, you'd think they'd be able to make Jesus taste better."

My 5 year old daughter and I were having a discussion the other day and she says to me...."You know mommy, when I'm a teenager and you're a grandma...." and then I passed out.

Chapter 6

Free to Forgive

Amy was watching her older sister, Lily, doing her chemistry homework when Amy asked "What's H20?" Lily explained "It's just a fancy way of saying water. The O stands for oxygen." Trying to show her older sister how smart she was, Amy interrupted "That makes sense. So the "H" must mean hose since that's what water comes out of."
(www.HeardonthePlayground.com)

I don't know how many times I've messed up in my life, but it has been way too many to count. Raising children seems to bring out the very best and worst in people. I know for me, things have never been the same since my first daughter came screaming into this world.

The principle of forgiveness is what initially sparked my interest in writing this book. I've never seen anyone on this earth display the virtue of forgiveness better than a child. Children know how to forgive, and they do it right. They are a great example for the world to see and from which to learn.

Spend a little time in a classroom full of young children and you'll see what I mean. Johnny is playing with little Brandon, and all of a sudden Johnny decides that he's going to hit Brandon over the head with this toy truck. He picks it up and wham! Right on Brandon's head.

Of course Brandon immediately goes crying to the teacher saying, "Johnny hit me!" But in a matter of minutes, the boys will be playing together again. It's remarkable how not even 5 minutes ago this little boy wronged Brandon, but Brandon has gotten over it to the point of trusting Johnny again, and they both continue on playing and being friends. It's that simple. The parents of the kids, on the other hand, might try to keep the two of them separated, because they think they know better and are trying to protect little Brandon. As we get older, things seem to get way more complicated...or do they?

Forgiveness Defined

So, what exactly is forgiveness? Forgiveness is defined in the dictionary as this: *to grant pardon for or remission of (an offense, debt, etc.).*
Another definition that's listed is: *to give up all claim on to of; remit(debt, obligation, etc.).* [13]
In both definitions there is an understanding of an outstanding debt that one party owes and that the other has decided to let go. This is exactly how it is in our lives. When someone wrongs us, no matter how big or small, we feel as if they owe us something. Maybe we feel like they owe us an apology or something even greater than that. Maybe you have a father who never was there, so you feel as if he owes you what you think being a good father should be. You feel that he owes you for the time he missed when he was not there when you were younger. If he doesn't deliver as you think he should, or maybe apologize for his absence in your childhood, you now feel you have a "right" to hold a

grudge or continually be hurt by him failing your expectations of what a good dad should be.

Or perhaps my mom always promised things to me and never delivered, so I feel as if she owes me being faithful to her word. Since she never delivered the way I thought she should growing up, she owes me something. There's a void *she* created and she needs to fill it somehow. She *should've done what she said*, and I'll hold it against her in my heart because she didn't. If something comes up between the two of us, I'll have ammunition to fire because of all the hurt she created in me.

Maybe your boyfriend decided to date your best friend, and they went behind your back in doing so, so they definitely owe you...and you still intend to get some kind of revenge when the time is right. There's no way you can let them get away with something that hurt so badly. How could they do that to you?

Sometimes we feel like we have a right to continue in our anger just because we've been hurt – no matter how badly. We tend to hold a grudge against the person who took out our heart and stomped on it. It makes sense not to forgive. It makes sense to continue feeling that you're right never to speak to the person who has hurt you again. That's what our hearts would say to do...but it's not what God says.

Forgiving others is not a one-time event. It's something that needs to be done over and over, in a lot of cases many times a day...you know, seventy-seven times? In Matt. 18:21, Peter comes to Jesus and asks, "Lord, how many times shall I forgive my brother when he sins against me? Up to seven times?" Jesus answered, "I tell you, not seven times, but seventy-seven times."

In my life I have to forgive my husband just about every single day, if not multiple times in a day. It's not necessarily because he's wronged me, I just feel like I'm entitled to certain things as a wife, when in fact, he owes me absolutely nothing.

I think to myself (and many times I'll blurt it out), "Why can't he pick up his clothes? I'm so tired of seeing a big pile of clothes when I know it's not that difficult to just put them away!"

One day as I was thinking this (or probably saying this out loud), Jesus clearly impressed upon my heart these words: "I pick up *your* clothes...." That's it. I was complaining about having to pick up after my husband, and Jesus convicted me. He has picked up, and continues to pick up all the messes that I make, *and* He never once has complained about it.

He certainly doesn't owe it to me, but He chooses to love me enough to forgive me. All the times that I've sinned against Him, He has removed my sins as far as the east is from the west, and we're to do nothing less with the people God has placed us with. I'm not saying that I don't complain anymore about Chris's clothes on the floor, its just that every time that the complaining comes to my mind and out of my mouth, I remember what Jesus said and did for me. Chris doesn't owe it to me to pick them up. In fact, he also owes me absolutely nothing.

Chris is one of the most gracious people I know. I know I'm constantly doing things that aggravate him, but I rarely hear it from him. Maybe it's just his personality, but he seems to just roll with whatever it is I do. If I mess up (which happens ALL the time) he immediately forgives me. I love that about my husband! I have never had a doubt of his love for me—even when I make so many mistakes.

You Must Forgive to be Forgiven

You might say to yourself, "Well, it's not that easy to forgive my husband. You don't know what he's done to me." It doesn't matter what he's done to you. He may have totally ruined your life in your eyes, but the Lord clearly says that if you don't forgive others, He won't forgive you. Period. If your heart is to follow God in this, then He most definitely sees your heart. However, if you choose to hold onto unforgiveness and bitterness when God tells you to let it go, you might want to be very careful. And the thing is, God ALWAYS tells us to let it go...even if we don't *feel* like it.

Jesus himself plainly says in Matthew 6:14-15, *"For if you forgive men when they sin against you, your heavenly Father will also forgive you. But if you do not forgive men their sins, your Father will not forgive your sins."*

Even in the Lord's prayer in Matthew 6:12, which so many pray on a regular basis, it says this: *"Forgive us our debts, as we also have forgiven our debtors."* Forgive us, *as* we've forgiven others. If we are still holding grudges, that's the degree to which we'll be forgiven.

So where does that leave us? The only answer is that we MUST forgive. It's NOT an option. If Jesus can forgive all that we've done against Him, it's not too much for Him to ask of us. He would not lead us down a road that He hasn't already walked down. He also doesn't lead us somewhere only to abandon us. He's with you all the time, empowering you to do what He's called you to do...to forgive.

I've seen through my ministry experience the power of forgiving. It truly sets you free. When you walk in unforgiveness, you are placing yourself in bondage but expecting that it will hurt the other person. Do you realize that when you forgive someone you're not only doing them a favor, but you're actually helping yourself? Forgiveness is a gift for everyone, especially the one who's doing the forgiving. I've heard many different quotes in regards to this:

"Unforgiveness is like a poison that you take, waiting for the other person to die."[14]

Or one of my personal favorites by Lewis B. Smedes:
"To forgive is to set a prisoner free and discover that the prisoner was you."

Time Heals ALL Wounds?

I'm sure you've heard many times that time heals all wounds. I completely disagree. Sure, time might make you feel better, but it doesn't truly heal. Forgiveness heals. Everyone in life has been hurt by someone at some point. Sometimes we choose to walk away from that person and that's the way we take care of the problem. Since we've removed ourselves from the situation, after some time has passed it feels like we don't have a problem with that person anymore.

This is all an illusion, kind of like a mirage in a desert. The pain that was caused by that person gets shoved down until it's buried beneath the cares of the world or any other things that might be going on. Then it happens again—someone hurts you and you push it down. Maybe this time you don't just leave, but you never really forgive. You just overlook it. Overlooking a problem seems like the best thing to do…however, it isn't. In many cases the offense needs to be addressed with the other person as you forgive so that there's clarity between you both. If it's not addressed, confusion and hurt can set in and destroy the relationship.

Of course in some instances it might be a situation where you need to take the offense to God only. I know for me I can be overly sensitive in certain relationships. I tend to read much deeper into something that was said or done, and my feelings will get hurt as a consequence. If I wait and take it to God, in many cases I end up realizing that my hurt came from my own insecurity. If it is a recurring feeling that I can't shake through prayer, then it definitely needs to be addressed with the other person.

The Bible says in Matthew 18:15 that "If your brother sins against you, go and show him his fault, just between the two of you. If he listens to you, you have won your brother over." If someone has sinned against me or hurt me, it's my job to gently confront them and let them know so that things don't get out of hand. It's NOT my job to go talk to everyone else about my issues and spread unnecessary gossip, or to hold it in and work through things on my own until it's pushed down enough for me to be around that person again. Although confrontation can be difficult, it is necessary for us to walk in freedom and forgiveness.

I remember talking with two different friends about managers at different job sites. These mangers had a problem with the way things were being done but would never communicate this problem to the employee. This is a very bad and unfair situation because the employee, in both of these instances, lost their job because of it.

Had the manager clearly communicated his expectations of the employee, there would be no confusion and the job might have gotten done properly. Had it been communicated and then the employee continued without making the necessary changes, there would then be grounds for letting the employee go.

I believe it works similarly in relationships and forgiveness. If I am hurt by someone and I don't communicate it to them, their actions won't change and I will continue getting hurt. They will have absolutely no idea that the way they are acting bothers me in the least. It needs to be confronted with a gentle spirit, not pointing fingers. In some cases that person might not be willing to change, and then you'll need to ask God for further direction on how to handle it from there. He might show you that you're being too sensitive, or perhaps, you might need to re-evaluate your relationship.

In Matthew 5:23-25, the Bible says this: "Therefore if you are offering your gift at the altar and there remember that your brother has something against you, leave your gift there in front of the altar. First go and be reconciled to your brother; then come and offer your gift. Settle matters quickly with your adversary...." It's so clear that God intends for us to be unified with each other. He wants us to live a life that is constantly forgiveness centered, loving each other through our faults. In this scripture it says that if you feel like your brother has something against *you,* not if you have something against your brother.

So it works both ways...if you have something against someone, it needs to be addressed. Or if you feel like they have *something against you*, you need to address it. If we, as Christians, would be adamant about this type of relational living, we'd see a huge change in our churches and even the culture. If we live in a constant state of forgiveness, mercy, and grace toward others, it would literally change the world around us. We all make mistakes, we all say things we shouldn't, and we all are imperfect human beings. God's plan is for us to always freely offer forgiveness to everyone.

No Time to Waste!

The key to forgiveness is that it is done as quickly as possible. The longer it goes before it's addressed, the more difficult it can become—not to mention it conveniently slips away and it's never truly dealt with. We need to be very adamant about this because if we don't forgive, we cannot live a life of freedom. Forgive immediately.

. A great quote I read recently is this:

True forgiveness is not an action after the fact, it is an attitude with which you enter each moment. – David Ridge

Knowing that people are going to mess up, you choose to forgive even before they make a mistake. *They don't, and never will, owe you anything.* That doesn't mean you'll never get hurt, or that you're putting up a wall. It only means that you know in your heart that no matter what happens, you will live a life of forgiveness towards everyone you meet. Not just the ones who treat you perfectly…Everyone.

We've all seen it happen and probably have had it happen within ourselves. Things just keep piling on and on until we finally can't take it anymore, and we blow up or walk away with lots of hurt and pain. Chances are the other person never really knows why. Unforgiveness is why most marriages and relationships end. There's nothing that's more detrimental in any relationship than unforgiveness.

My kids always have amazed me by the way they constantly and quickly forgive me. On numerous occasions the stress of life has overwhelmed me and I've found myself blowing up...and most of the time it's been at them—even though they aren't always the cause of my frustration (notice I said always). Since they are around they tend to receive the brunt of my emotional blowups.

I've yelled at my children more times than I can count, and I'm not happy that it's happened that way. The amazing thing, though, is that as I admit that I'm wrong, every single time they forgive me...no questions asked. I could have just said something incredibly harsh and made one of them cry because I'm having a bad day, but as soon as I ask for forgiveness and admit my guilt, they forgive. They hug me and let me know that they still love me. What an amazing example of Christ they are!

Here is an incredible example of how forgiveness not only impacted a local community, but the world:

> *On Monday morning, October 2, 2006, a gunman entered a one-room Amish school in Nickel Mines, Pennsylvania. In front of twenty-five horrified pupils, thirty-two-year-old Charles Roberts ordered the boys and the teacher to leave. After tying the legs of the ten remaining girls, Roberts prepared to shoot them execution style with an automatic rifle and four hundred rounds of ammunition that he brought for the task. The oldest hostage, a thirteen year old, begged Roberts to "shoot me first and let the little ones go." Refusing her offer, he opened fire on all of them, killing five and leaving the others critically wounded. He then shot himself as police stormed the building. His motivation? "I'm angry at God for taking my little daughter," he told the children before the massacre.*

The story captured the attention of broadcast and print media in the United States and around the world. By Tuesday morning some fifty television crews had clogged the small village of Nickel Mines, staying for five days until the killer and the killed were buried. The blood was barely dry on the schoolhouse floor when Amish parents brought words of forgiveness to the family of the one who had slain their children.

The outside world was incredulous that such forgiveness could be offered so quickly for such a heinous crime. Of the hundreds of media queries that the authors received about the shooting, questions about forgiveness rose to the top. Forgiveness, in fact, eclipsed the tragic story, trumping the violence and arresting the world's attention.

Within a week of the murders, Amish forgiveness was a central theme in more than 2,400 news stories around the world. The Washington Post, The New York Times, USA Today, Newsweek, NBC Nightly News, CBS Morning News, Larry King Live, Fox News, Oprah, and dozens of other media outlets heralded the forgiving Amish. From the Khaleej Times (United Arab Emirates) to Australian television, international media were opining on Amish forgiveness. Three weeks after the shooting, "Amish forgiveness" had appeared in 2,900 news stories worldwide and on 534,000 web sites.

Fresh from the funerals where they had buried their own children, grieving Amish families accounted for half of the seventy-five people who attended the killer's burial. Roberts' widow was deeply moved by their presence as Amish families greeted her and her three children. The forgiveness

*went beyond talk and graveside presence: the Amish
also supported a fund for the shooter's family.*[15]

This story is an amazing example of how Christ
desires for us to live. These people were obviously in
deep pain over the tragedy that occurred, but chose the
way of Christ in the midst of their pain. Not only did
they *say* they forgave the man, they *lived* it out in their
actions. Not to mention they forgave immediately.
Could they have held a grudge? Would they have been
justified to be angry? In the world's eyes, absolutely.
But not in the eyes of the one who forgave us. They
knew the power of what forgiveness brings. They knew
the healing and wholeness that it creates, and they
didn't want to wait any longer to obey the will of God,
no matter how difficult it was.

What is even more amazing than this is that Jesus
forgives us. No matter what we do or have done, His
blood and forgiveness is enough for every single person
that has ever walked or will walk upon this earth.

Let's decide today to choose to forgive quickly.
Let go of any grudges and remember to "Let no debt
remain outstanding, except the continuing debt to love
one another, for he who loves his fellowman has fulfilled
the law." Romans 13:8. Remember, no one ever owes
you anything.

JAMES (age 4) was listening to a Bible story. His dad read: "The man named Lot was warned to take his wife and flee out of the city but his wife looked back and was turned to salt." Concerned, James asked: "What happened to the flea?"

My son Bennett had learned about Adam and Eve at church on Sunday in his class and colored a picture of a snake in a tree...when he left class he ran up to my husband and said, "Happy Fathers Day Daddy, I made you a picture of Satan."

Before bed the other night I was washing my 4 year old son's feet in the bathroom sink and he said "Wow Mom, you must be Jesus because you're washing my feet!" - to which his twin sister immediately responded (in a voice of exasperation), "No she's not Jesus, He had a smaller towel".

Chapter 7

Free to Ask

Simon (after being in bed for 30 min); Mom, come on up! My back is itching.
Mom: You need to scratch it yourself.
Simon: I'm too busy right now!

Mommy, will you help me? Mommy, can you come here? Mommy, I'm thirsty, will you get me a drink?

These are questions my children repeat pretty much every single day about a hundred times. Help, Mommy, I can't tie my shoe! Help, I don't know what color that should be. Daddy, can you fix my toy? Kids definitely are NOT afraid to ask others when they need help. Not at all. In fact, they seem to announce it to the entire world when they can't do something they want to do or when they're not feeling their best. Everyone in the nearby vicinity seems to know when a child is in need of something. They are *never* afraid to ask. Even when they get turned down about 90% of the time, they still ask. I love that about them.

It seems that as we grow older we begin to hide what we really need. We feel ashamed when we can't do something without anyone else's help. If we're going through a rough time we just endure it and think to ourselves, "I don't want to bother anyone else with this problem. They have enough on their plate without needing to help me, too."

I've been in that situation more than once. I don't know why, but asking for help is so humbling—most likely because it exposes our weaknesses. The fact that we don't ask for help more often makes no sense to me. God put us here to help one another and encourage each other. Why not ask for help when things get tough? Why not admit that you can't do everything all by yourself? When you're down, why not ask a friend to lunch or call someone and ask for prayer? I've gotten much better at this through the years, and I would not be where I am today if I hadn't asked for help along the way.

A scripture that I hold onto and share with others on a regular basis is Galatians 6:2. It says, "Bear one another's burdens and in this way you will fulfill the law of Christ." We are meant to help one another. It's just a simple fact. Ecclesiastes 4:9 says, "Two are better than one because they have a good return for their work."

We need each other. We need help. We can't live life alone and at the same time be all that God has called us to be. We can't hide under the façade that everything is okay all the time. When things get tough, ask for help. It's amazing how much faster you'll rise out of the muck when you have someone to help lift you out. Climbing out alone is tedious and it's not what God intended. Most of the time we won't be able to get out unless we ask for help from someone else. And when we ask, we must be willing to receive the help that's offered, too.

My Story

That's precisely where I was in life for many years. I was stuck in a major rut; I didn't know who to turn to for help, so I just stayed there having no idea how to get out.

When I was a campus minister at North Carolina State my life had an appearance of being very well put together. I had a great husband who loved me, three amazing children who were all healthy (and slept through the night, might I add!), and a campus ministry that was successful. My parents would even come up once a week so I could go to the large group ministry meetings on campus to help out. I felt called to be in ministry and had been doing it for many years at this point, but for some reason I was not happy at all in my life.

When I was at home I'd find myself getting upset at my children, yelling at my husband, and just being an unpleasant person to be around. I felt like a failure, because I had it in my mind that someone like me, a Christian, and on top of that a vocational minister, should never yell at their kids like I did. I should have had everything under control, being joyful in all circumstances while encouraging others around me. Well, I sure had everyone fooled, didn't I? In the midst of it all I still met with students for mentoring and Bible studies.

When I finished encouraging other people, I'd go home, not wanting to be there. I didn't have my laundry put away, the kids' rooms were a mess, and the kitchen still needed to be cleaned from the last meal. There was always something that was hanging over my head. If I was a *good* wife, I'd have all of this under control. I'd look around at other ladies who were my age, and they appeared as if everything was neatly put together in their lives. Somehow in the midst of all they had to do, they could mop their floors on a regular basis and never have laundry piles to fold and put away. Why was it so easy for them, yet so difficult for me?

Everywhere I turned when I was at home I felt like a failure. Since I constantly was feeling bad about myself I'd get upset extremely easily with the kids and of course, with Chris. After all, in my mind he was the main problem. Why couldn't he help more around the house? Couldn't he see that I can't do it by myself? Of course I was wrong in thinking this way about him. It became a horrible cycle that I could not pull myself out of. I was in a downward spiral and couldn't get out by myself.

I would spend time with the Lord and feel encouraged that I could do it all, but later on that same day I'd find myself screaming at the kids again for something that wasn't even that big of a deal, or I'd be getting on Chris for just about anything he did. It seemed like he could just be breathing, and I would jump on his case. I wondered if this cycle would ever come to an end. I knew that this wasn't God's "life of abundance" that He promised, and I didn't know if I'd ever experience it again.

A women's retreat was coming up at church, and there is never a time when I don't absolutely LOVE going away with a group of ladies to the mountains! I was going to be leading worship for this retreat, and so I was getting excited and hopeful about what God might do there. Unfortunately I ended up with a terrible cold and lost my voice on the drive up, but somehow God still used me to lead worship with the much needed help of some of the other ladies.

While I was on the retreat, there was an hour long session of "soaking prayer" scheduled for Saturday morning after the first session. I had vaguely heard of it before, but I assumed it was something that I knew I'd enjoy.

That morning I woke up early enough to go out for a walk in the beautiful mountains of North Carolina. It was amazing watching the sunrise and spending some time with Jesus. During that time I was pouring my heart out to the Lord and telling Him how much I needed Him to help me. I obviously couldn't do this thing on my own, and so I went down a list of things with Him that was on my mind. All of my fears and failures, hurts, and uncertainties were among the main things that I shared with God. I needed him desperately, and so I cried out. It was a good time with the Lord, but I had prayed the same prayer before, so I wasn't sure what to expect.

Later that day I went to the soaking prayer session. It was amazing what God did in my heart during that time. If you don't know what soaking prayer is, it's a time where you sit in silence before the Lord and "soak" in his presence. We lay down with blankets and pillows and turned off all the lights. Worship music played while we were on the floor in the dark, so it was very peaceful and relaxing.

As soon as the lights went out, tears came to my eyes and started rolling down my face. I was scared because I didn't know what to do. I had let God down, so I thought, and I didn't know how to make it right. A few minutes into the soaking, the lady who was leading the session, Holly, came over and began to pray for me. I had never met her or spoken to her before, but God ministered so powerfully through her, and she directly touched on every detail that I had just talked to God about earlier that morning. Every single one. I knew God heard my prayer and was telling me of His great love for me.

Tears were streaming down my face, and what touched me so deeply was that Holly was crying also. A person whom I'd never met before had such compassion towards me and for what was going on in my life. She didn't know me, but she still had an amazing amount of love and mercy for me and for all I was going through. The compassion that she displayed was something that I had desired for so long in my life, yet I never seemed to have it. The fact that she would hear God so clearly and allow Him to minister through her with such great love and concern cut me to the core.

After soaking prayer was over I did not want to go anywhere. God had met me in such a powerful way, and I finally believed that I could, with His grace, overcome what I'd been dealing with for so long. After I went home from the weekend, I realized that I couldn't walk the path of faith by myself. I needed help, and I needed to ask, just like our three-year-old friends would.

I knew that Holly had a type of compassion and mercy for others that I had been longing for, so I sought her out. I emailed Holly, and we started to get together on a regular basis. Through talking and prayer with her, and eventually attending a week long ministry called "Restoring the Foundations," God brought me out of the rut that I had lived in for so long. It was an amazing time, but the key to all of it was that I couldn't do it alone. I had to ask for help. I had to ask God for help, and I had to ask others for help also. I had to ask for prayer. I had to admit that I couldn't overcome this battle by myself, and when I finally was humble and open enough to allow someone in to help me, things quickly started looking up.

Confess and Ask

James 5:16 says, "Therefore confess your sins to each other and pray for each other so that you may be healed. The prayer of a righteous man is powerful and effective." This scripture is absolutely true. I needed to confess my unbelief. I needed to be vulnerable and not to be so prideful about the struggles that I was going through. In order for me to receive healing in this area of my life, confession was necessary, just like James says.

The enemy loves to keep things hidden. He knows that when we are hiding things, there is no way we can have victory. We can't overcome by ourselves. He deceives us into thinking that others won't accept us if they knew what was going on in our lives. That's not the truth at all. We will remain in bondage unless we follow this command to confess to one another and to pray for each other. There is no other way. You must face your problems with God and others. There are no shortcuts.

This principle obviously applies with Jesus as well. Many times we won't even ask Him for the help that we need. We try to figure out the answers to all of our problems first, and when we can't do it ourselves, then we might decide to ask the Lord. Sometimes we actually never get around to asking Him because we don't even think about it. That leads me to believe that deep down in our hearts, we don't think that Jesus will respond. We say that prayer works and that He answers prayer, but if we believed it, why would anything keep us from asking?

He truly is the answer. He is the one we need in every area of our lives. He is our sustainer. Just because He might not answer our prayer the exact way we want Him to doesn't mean that He doesn't know best or that

He doesn't hear us. He always knows best. Sometimes He's just making sure that we ask, and many times we don't. James 4:2b says, "You do not have because you do not ask God." We need not be afraid of coming to Jesus and asking for the help we need.

Earlier in James 1:5-7 it says:

If any of you lacks wisdom, he should ask God, who gives generously to all without finding fault, and it will be given to him. 6 But when he asks, he must believe and not doubt, because he who doubts is like a wave of the sea, blown and tossed by the wind. 7 That man should not think he will receive anything from the Lord; 8 he is a double-minded man, unstable in all he does."

Asking for help is exactly the place God wants us. He wants us to be humbly dependent on Him. When we go to Him we must know without a doubt that He will answer us. He is faithful. He is true. He loves you more than you could ever imagine, and it is His privilege to bless His children with the help they need...and even way more than that. He blesses us with his amazing presence.

This is the confidence we have in approaching God: that if we ask anything according to his will, he hears us.15 And if we know that he hears us – whatever we ask – we know that we have what we asked of him. 1 John 5:14-15

What an amazing promise! God hears us and answers faithfully. We need not be afraid to ask.

Here is a great story illustrating our need to not be afraid to ask for help.

A little boy was spending his Saturday morning playing in his sandbox. He had with him his box of cars and trucks, his plastic pail, and a shiny, red plastic shovel.

In the process of creating roads and tunnels in the soft sand, he discovered a large rock in the middle of the sandbox.

The boy dug around the rock, managing to dislodge it from the dirt. With a little bit of struggle, he pushed and nudged the large rock across the sandbox by using his feet.

When the boy got the rock to the edge of the sandbox, he found that he couldn't roll it up and over the wall of the sandbox.

Determined, the little boy shoved, pushed, and pried, but every time he thought he had made some progress, the rock tipped and then fell back into the sandbox.

The little boy grunted, struggled, pushed, and shoved, but his only reward was to have the rock roll back, smashing his chubby fingers.

Finally he burst into tears of frustration. All this time the boy's father watched from his living room window as the drama unfolded. At the moment the tears fell, a large shadow fell across the boy and the sandbox.

It was the boy's father. Gently but firmly he said, "Son, why didn't you use all the strength that you had available?"

Defeated, the boy sobbed back, "But I did, Daddy, I did! I used all the strength that I had!"

"No, son," corrected the father kindly. "You didn't use all the strength you had. You didn't ask me."

With that the father reached down, picked up the rock and removed it from the sandbox.[16]

What a picture this is of our heavenly Father. We try and try to move the rocks in our lives and take care of everything ourselves. So many times though when we ask and the answer comes, we are unwilling to receive it. If we'd humble ourselves like a child and just ask and receive He'd come and move it for us. What an amazing God and Father we serve.

Asking for and Receiving Forgiveness

In the last chapter we talked about forgiving others, but asking for and being on the receiving end of forgiveness is another story. Just as no one ever owes you anything, *you also* don't owe anyone anything…just love (Rom. 13:8). On many occasions as I had to face my children and ask their forgiveness, I felt completely unworthy to be forgiven because of the way I had acted. I was no better than a worm in my eyes, and I had no right to even be their mother because of how badly I felt I was messing it up.

Even though forgiveness was graciously extended to me, I, because of my great guilt, rejected it and continued to feel bad about myself. I felt like I didn't deserve it and what I really deserved was a much greater punishment than that, so I chose not to let it go. Part of asking for forgiveness is actually receiving it when it's given.

Somehow we feel that there's no way we could get off so easily when we've messed up so badly. But the truth is it IS that easy. Receiving forgiveness doesn't necessarily reverse our actions or the wrong we've done, it just wipes the slate clean to give us another chance. And yes, it's completely clean. There aren't any left over marks on it from when we messed up before. When we're forgiven, it's for forever. It's a gift, and it takes humility and vulnerability to receive it.

When we receive forgiveness, we're admitting that we're wrong, but indeed it's not too great for God to repair. He knows that there are temptations and struggles, and He knows our weaknesses even more than we do. Feeling as if we don't deserve to be forgiven is a lie from the enemy to keep us in chains. We, in ourselves, don't deserve it; however, Jesus does, and He lives inside of us and He makes us COMPLETELY worthy to receive forgiveness. And when we do allow ourselves to receive it, we can get up and move on. We don't have to stay down any longer. We can continue running this race guilt-free because of all that Christ has done for us.

When I finally caught a glimpse of this promise for real, it was like the chains fell to the ground. I had been living as a Christian for so many years, beating myself up constantly but for what? What a tactic of the enemy! He wants us to feel unworthy so we don't ever finish the race that God has set before us.

How is it that I could possibly be "good enough" to do something so great, Lord? How is it that You've called me to be a mother, when I'm such a failure? Why would I ever be able to lead a Bible study group when my life is in shambles? Why is it that we have such a hard time moving on when we struggle? Why is it so difficult to receive the forgiveness that's completely free for us to receive? All I know is that the devil is the only one who doesn't want you to keep moving forward, and he'll do anything in his power to keep your mind going in the wrong direction.

Thinking that you're unworthy of forgiveness is a major form of pride. It's self-focused, not God-focused. It becomes all about you, not about God. Yes, sin is not good, but Jesus has already pardoned it for you. You're set free in Him. There's nothing more you can do.

He's the one who made me, and He's the one who made this deal for me, so who am I not to believe it? Who am I to think that I'm the one person who's so bad that I don't deserve what Christ has readily offered on the cross? When you mess up, repent, ask for forgiveness and then get right back up. The finish line is waiting for you, and there's a great cloud of witnesses there to cheer you on (Hebrews 12:1).

Now, flip the coin for a moment. On the other side of this coin is what's called trampling on the grace of God (see Romans 6). While some of us might have major difficulty receiving forgiveness, others might have the problem of having no contrition in their heart. They sin and never ask forgiveness, or they sin and don't think anything of it because they know that they'll be forgiven. This quote hits on this topic:

"When I was a kid I used to pray every night for a new bicycle. Then I realized that the Lord doesn't work that way so I stole one and asked Him to forgive me." – Emo Philips

This is a very clear example of trampling on God's grace. Paul obviously warns about this in scripture. We need to have a broken and contrite heart towards God and our sin. If we don't, we need to ask

God to give us a broken and contrite heart; otherwise our hearts might become hard in our relationship with Jesus. We need to fear God. He always knows our motives, and when the end comes, He will judge us accordingly.

Like I've said, it's vitally important to ask for and receive the forgiveness God offers with open arms, choosing to not stay down in our race...but it's also important to know our place, and that's to love and follow God with our whole heart, doing our best to live according to His word. The great thing is, we cannot do this thing in our own strength. We have the power of the almighty God living inside of us, and by His grace we can be all that He's called and equipped us to be...if we'll just receive it and believe it.

Children aren't afraid to ask for anything at all. They ask big. They ask for help. They receive forgiveness. God wants to help us, to hold us, and to love us, and He promises to meet our every need. Don't be afraid to ask for or receive anything He has to give. One of my favorite scriptures is Ephesians 3:20: "Now to Him who is able to do immeasurably **more** than all we ask or imagine..." He can do anything...don't be afraid to ask. You're worth it!

Part 3

Free to Love!

As we were passing by a field with a many cows, I said, "Wow, look at all of those cow patties out there!" My 7 year old daughter replies, "Where? I don't see any hamburgers out there." I had to explain that cow patties were NOT the same as hamburgers...

From my 3-year-old daughter, "Mommy, I love you so very much, but you need to go away for right now. I need 'me' time.

My then three-year old asked me for a snack. I said "No, because you had snacks left and right at the softball game tonight." She asked, "Was the popcorn on the left and the pretzels on the right?

Chapter 8

Free to Cry

During a sad part of a movie, my son whispered to himself, "Stop, man. Hold it in, you can do it." His eyes were welling up with tears. When he noticed me looking he said, "What? I'm not crying, my eyes are just sweating." Dylan, 9 (HeardonthePlayground.com)

Tears. Some hate shedding them; some don't mind it at all. Tears come easily to many, yet others have such a difficult time letting them flow even when times get tough. Why? What makes us so different from one another when it comes to showing emotion?

Children seem to all be the same when it comes to tears. They let them go no matter what the circumstance. They cry when they get hurt, they cry when someone is mean to them, they cry when they miss their mommy, and many times they cry very loudly when they don't get what they want. If tears come easily for them, why is crying so difficult for many of us?

I knew so many people who would cry no matter what was going on. They'd go to a movie and cry through the whole thing. I'd kind of laugh to myself and think. "What in the world are they crying about? It's just a movie! There's no reason to sit here and sob when it's just a story!" People would cry at weddings, at graduations, and if their dog died. I never got it, until Jesus showed me otherwise.

Jesus Wept

This one scripture alone has been known for being the shortest, easiest verse in the Bible. If you ever want to memorize a scripture, here it is: John 11:35, "Jesus wept."

It wasn't until a short time ago that I truly understood the power of those words. Jesus, the son of God, Creator of the world and everything in it, the One who knows all the hairs on my head, who flung the stars into the sky, and who is bigger and more powerful than any other….He wept. Why in the world would the man, God, have any need in weeping? Why would He show this apparent weakness (at least the world might call it that)?

I grew up in a home where we never talked openly about our feelings, and I never felt as if I could open up my heart to anyone. Like I mentioned earlier, I always wanted to be able to cry, but I never felt released to do so. I had to be the strong one, I mean, after all there was nothing to cry about, right? Nothing could possibly be so wrong in my life that I would need to shed any tears over it. Obviously that train of thought was completely incorrect.

As I was spending time with Jesus one evening, He reassured me that it's okay to be broken. It's okay to let your heart be vulnerable. In fact, these were the moments when God seemed to touch my heart the deepest. It's okay to weep. After all, Jesus wept. Jesus, the king of all kings, had reason to shed tears, and so do I.

This passage is telling the story of when Jesus came to visit Mary, Martha, and Lazarus's house after a long journey. He waited two extra days before He decided to go, knowing all along that Lazarus was sick to the point of death. When He arrived, the sisters and all the Jews that were there were in tears. They had lost their brother and friend, so their hearts were broken.

This is the good part...Jesus wept with them. This man who had all the answers, the power to heal and raise from the dead, took time to weep with those who were weeping. He had compassion on them and displayed just how deep His love extended to those who were hurting. He didn't correct or rebuke. He didn't even raise Lazarus immediately. He wept. This hit me, and it hit me hard. If Jesus weeps, then I can feel free to do the same. What an amazing man!

Crying...Not So Easy for Me!

I know for me, the thought of shedding tears has always been a weakness. I never wanted to cry around anyone because I feared that they would think I was trying to get attention or that I was being a wimp. If I cried, it showed weakness – showing people that I wasn't as strong as they thought I was. I always had it together. Even if life got tough for me, I was still strong and had faith that God was in control. Nothing at all was really a big deal.

No matter what the circumstance was that was coming at me, I refused to shed any tears. Not in front of a person anyway, unless, of course I was at a funeral. And you should only really shed tears at a funeral if it's someone that you were close to. You don't have the right to be sad if it's someone you only knew for a short while. Besides, I didn't have any right to be sad because the family were the ones who would miss that person the most, not me.

In reality, however, deep down I wanted to be able to cry. I wanted to let out my emotions in front of people so that they could comfort me and know what was really going on in my life. I wanted to cry on someone's shoulder and allow that person to love me, despite what I was going through. I desperately needed someone to affirm me and hold me and tell me just how much I meant to them. Why wouldn't I just let it out, then?

I know when I'm broken, many times I'll try to talk myself out of it. I'll feel like a failure, as if I should have had more faith, or I'll feel as if something so trite shouldn't have affected me so deeply. All I know is that when I've been in tears through various seasons of life, God has met me. He has shown me His compassion. He has wept with me, held me, and been more patient with me in my struggles than I could ever have hoped.

One evening as I was praying, I felt His presence right there with me. He was encouraging me by telling me that it doesn't stop with Him simply weeping with me. He weeps with us, shows us deep compassion, and then what happens after that? He raises the dead! All these trials, all the brokenness, all the pain...what does it end in? A resurrection! One that no one was expecting. After all, Lazarus had been dead for 4 days. Wow. God is just like that. One day we're broken, crying out, and the next moment God comes in and resurrects the dead. He lifts us out of our brokenness, touches our heart, and sets us free. He takes the place in our heart and restores it. He takes our situation and completely makes it new. What an amazing, compassionate, powerful, resurrecting God we serve.

Being free to shed tears is a sign of strength, not weakness. To be vulnerable enough to allow someone to see your weakness is total strength.

I know for me, it wasn't until recently that I realized the importance of allowing myself to cry…to let tears flow when they needed to. I spent most of my life pushing down my feelings and tears. I've found out, however, it's when I allow them to fall that healing comes. Even if it's something small, unimportant, or something you don't think you should be affected by, it doesn't matter. Letting out your emotion brings healing. Crying on God's shoulder enables a new sense of acceptance and relief that pushing the emotions down or ignoring them will not.

I was talking with a friend the other day about this. She is a definite crier. I love it. I've gone to a few movies with her, sat through some Bible studies, and been in some other situations and she has no shame in this area whatsoever. Her husband even mentioned that she cried when they went on a date and saw the movie "Men in Black 3." Not exactly a movie you'd think people would be crying in, but she did. I think it's fantastic for her to be able to let her emotions show. That's exactly what children do. They let it flow when they feel it. And you know what? You feel much better after letting it out.

Being Broken

This year has been one of the hardest years I've ever been through. I don't know exactly what God has in store for my family, but all I know is that if a test brings a testimony, then I'll have a big one coming my way in the future.

About a year ago Chris and I decided to make a very difficult decision to step away from a church we dearly loved in order to take over an existing church that was struggling. In fact, there was only one couple left who was committed to being there. It was in the area, so thankfully we didn't have to move or leave our friends behind.

Church planting has been something we have felt called to do together even before we were married. It has been on Chris's heart for years and so much of what he thought about, planned, and dreamed of consisted of the church that God one day would birth through us.

We considered the church we took over basically a church plant since there were so few members left. We changed the name and started to work very hard at building it according to what we believed was God's direction. It was not an easy time at all because Chris was not only trying to pastor a church plant, he was also working a full-time job as well in addition to being a good husband and father. We plugged away for about 8 months, doing everything we knew to do to help get the church off the ground. We prayed. We believed. We fasted. Many people visited, but for some reason no one was "sticking."

We finally had to pray about shutting it down, and that is what we felt led to do. It took a lot of faith to close the doors. It was a successful time in that we saw some people come to Christ; however, it didn't feel very successful in our hearts. We were broken and confused. We ended up going back to the church we left, which I now know is where we needed to be.

In the midst of the church plant ending, my lower back started giving me problems. I was doing a very intense workout one day and ended up damaging a disc in my back. I thought I was better the next day and decided to lift a very heavy ladder and try to load it in the car. That was the end of it. I couldn't move after that. I was in excruciating pain that shot down my right leg into my foot. I couldn't stand up straight or get in any position that made it feel better. I called Chris at work, and he came home and ended up taking me to a chiropractor.

After about three months passed, I ended up needing back surgery. On top of all of this, with the church ending our financial situation became very difficult as well. Thankfully Chris still had his full-time job, but we didn't have enough to pay all of our bills. It was the first time we'd ever gotten behind on any of it, and it was very stressful. The devil tried to convince us that we were failures everywhere we turned.

Some relationship problems with friends came as well, which of course broke my heart again. If that weren't enough, my parents, who had been living about an hour away from us, decided it was time to move closer to their parents ten hours away.

Everywhere we looked things were driving us to our knees. I never felt like we'd ever escape this season. Right now we're still in the midst of some of the hardships from this time, but I have to say God is meeting us here. He's helping me to realize how He deeply cares about me and that will never leave me or forsake me. He's showing me that joy doesn't only come in the good times, but it also comes in the bad times. Strength is building up on the inside like I've never experienced before. It's real. It's not based on what I think I know. I actually know now what it means to be broken...and it hurts! But I've found God here in a way I never had in the past.

I've never leaned on others as much as I have during this time. I have a small group ladies Bible study that I'm a part of, and every single one of those women have been such a support to me. I've cried and cried more than I ever had, wondering when it will ever end. They have each encouraged me, brought me meals when my back was hurting, and prayed with me through this time. They have seen the best and worst of me...and they still love me.

I have to say that I have not been afraid to cry during this time. I've let tears fall when they needed to, just about every day for the majority of a year, and you know what? It feels good. It feels like I've released my pain to the One who can handle it and help me through it. He might not take all the problems away, but He walks with me through them. I know He's right here, shedding His compassionate tears with me, just like He did with Mary and Martha when their brother died.

"What is it about tears that should be so terrifying? the touch of God is marked by tears...deep, soul-shaking tears, weeping...it comes when that last barrier is down and you surrender yourself to health and wholeness"[17]

–David R. Wilkerson, "The Cross and the Switchblade"

I am thankful now, more than ever, for brokenness. For tears. I'm thankful that I have the ability to shed them and that with each one that falls, a deeper level of healing takes place. I can't imagine how I would feel right now if I had bottled them up through all of this. I think I would have probably exploded!

Brokenness, as painful as it is, is a gift. Just as the good times are a gift, God uses the bad times to draw us deeper. And when we go deeper with Jesus there is a supernatural strength and love that no one will ever be able to take away from us. When we've been through it, we can guide others through those times as well, knowing that God is faithful.

You always feel better when you've had a good cry. Just ask a 3 year old. It's great for you to let it out. Tears of joy, sadness, pain or compassion. Let them flow. Jesus did, and what an example for us He set.

Joey, one of my students, was absent from school. When he returned the next day he handed me a note. I read the note and asked what was wrong. He replied, "I don't know." Confused I said, "But your note says you saw the doctor." Joey answered, "Yeah, but I couldn't understand a word he said." "Why?" I asked. Joey replied arnestly, "Isn't it obvious?....I don't speak cursive yet." (www.HeardonthePlayground.com)

Driving in the car, my 2 year old asked if we run out of gas can we call the hooker? (tow truck)

My 4 year old daughter and her two cousins, 4 & 6yrs old, were playing in her room one day when I overheard them bickering. The 4 year old cousin had wanted to play with a toy and my daughter didn't want to share. Eddi Rose said, "No Legacy, you can't play with it, it is expensive!" (Which it was not) I went in and asked her "Eddi, do you know what expensive means?" Her reply, "Yes, It means nobody can mess with it!

Chapter 9

Free to Love the Unlovable

TAMMY (age 4) was with her mother when they met an elderly, rather wrinkled woman her Mom knew. Tammy looked at her for a while and then asked, "Why doesn't your skin fit your face?" (HeardonthePlayground.com)

Wholeness is a word that never made sense to me. What does it really mean to be whole? I certainly don't want to have pieces missing or anything "wrong" with me. It is the desire of God for us to walk in wholeness as we follow Christ.

As crazy as this sounds, little kids display wholeness to me all the time. They have the capacity to do so much and live life to the fullest, not worrying about anything else. They forgive when needed, dance when they feel like it, and crash when they need to.

One thing children do that amazes me is how they love the people that so many of us would consider "unlovable." It doesn't matter if their grandmother has a beard, they will love that woman no matter what. It doesn't matter if their mom has chronic halitosis, they don't care. Sure, they might tell their mom, but their love for her never changes. Hugs never cease. It doesn't matter how big you are, what the color of your hair might be (if you even have hair), or what your skin color is. They might ask why someone looks different, but they still love that person and accept them for who they are.

I find it funny sometimes how we, as parents, tend to ask our kids to give a hug to someone when we're telling them goodbye. Most of the time the parent never even does it! But it doesn't matter who the person is that a child is asked to hug…they just do it, unless of course they are afraid.

Showing No Favoritism

I remember going to someone's home, and it wasn't the nicest home (at least from my perspective). My daughter Hope could have cared less. She kept asking when we'd get to go back and kept saying just how great of a place it was. It didn't matter to her where it was located or how big it was. She loved it anyway. She didn't think less of the person who lived there because of the size of her home or how messy it was. What a characteristic! What a great trait to have—and we are all called to live this way. The way Hope loved in this situation obviously showed that it didn't matter to her how much the other person had or the way they kept their house; she would love them anyway.

Jesus hated when people were shown preference because of an outward trait. He made it clear that we are not supposed to show favor to the ones who have more money or look a certain way. In James chapter 2 it says:

"My brothers, as believers in our glorious Lord Jesus Christ, don't show favoritism. ² Suppose a man comes into your meeting wearing a gold ring and fine clothes, and a poor man in shabby clothes also comes in. ³ If you show special attention to the man wearing fine clothes and say, "Here's a good seat for you," but say to the poor man, "You stand there" or "Sit on the floor by my feet," ⁴ have you not discriminated among yourselves and become judges with evil thoughts?"
(James 2:1-4, NIV)

What exactly is favoritism? As humans we have a tendency to "judge a book by its cover." When we look at someone, we immediately make a judgment call on who we think that person might be or what they might act like, etc.

I don't think there are too many Western Christians that don't tend to do this. Just look at our churches. I've heard it said many times that Sunday mornings are the most segregated times of the week. We look at one another and notice that we're not alike, so we tend to shy away from each other and think that we probably won't get along. I'm not saying that churches are bad for not being diverse, but it does make you think a little bit as to why it is this way.

Not only are churches not diverse in their skin color, they are also not diverse in their socio-economic status. Most of the time you have the same "class" of people going to the same type of church. It makes sense that we naturally gravitate towards people like ourselves. The question however is, "What did Jesus do?"

He loved the unlovable. Jesus reached out to those whom the world had scorned as unworthy. Jesus associated with those who were different than He was. Jesus offered hope where there was no hope, peace where there was no peace, and joy where there was no joy. He offered the love of the Father to the people who needed it most. He didn't come to save the "saved." He came to save the lost.

That is exactly what we're called to do as believers. We're called to reach out to the ones who need us the most. The ones who are hurting, broken, and desperate for any kind of touch from God. The children who are orphans without a mom or a dad to love them. The fatherless, the widows, the poor, and the needy. That is why it is so important for us to live a life of wholeness ourselves. How can we extend the peace of Jesus to others if we're not walking in it ourselves? How can we tell someone about how great our God is if we've not truly experienced His greatness?

Jesus Loves Us When We're Unlovable

I once heard a quote that took me a while to swallow: "All introspection is sin." I wasn't sure what to think of it at first. I dwelt on it for a while and came to realize that I believe it is true. I'm not at all saying that we don't need to examine ourselves according to the Word of God, because we are instructed to do just that in the book of 2 Corinthians 13:5. We are to examine ourselves to see if we are in the faith. It's good to look within our hearts and test it to see if we indeed are living according to the word of God. Introspection that isn't led by the Holy Spirit is self-fulfilling and not God focused.

For me, examining myself in light of what God says about me was a huge step to wholeness. I'm not saying that I live a perfectly whole life, but it sure is much better than what it used to be. God took me through a season where He weeded out so much stuff that wasn't Him, and it was amazing. He cared enough about unlovable me, that He took the time to clean me up.

When we become Christians, we are immediately given the rights to all the promises of God. We are set free by Christ, and we'll be living with Him in eternity. We are children of God as soon as we confess Jesus as lord of our lives. Why then was it almost 20 years later that God took me through this process of weeding out the bad? Why is it that most Christians these days aren't walking in the freedom God has for them?

Jesus died to set us free and make us whole. He didn't die on the cross so we could live a mediocre life. He died so we could live, not just get by. He died so God would be glorified and so that we could be united with Him. He gave us all authority over the things of this world. All authority! He has overcome the world! (John 16:33) We might have trouble in the world, but the One who has overcome it lives inside of us. That makes us overcomers. The One who is in me is greater than the one who is in the world! (1 Jn 4:4).

He loves to see His children walk in freedom and wholeness; otherwise, Christ died for nothing. He didn't just die for us so we could go to heaven one day. Eternity starts right now...here in our lives on earth. Knowing Jesus, as mentioned in John 17:3, is the beginning of our eternal life.

If you're not living a life that outwardly displays these things, it might be time to do some examining of your heart in light of God's word to see what's going on. The great thing is that God values you so much that He takes all the time needed to show you where you need His freedom so you can walk in the authority that He's given to you. He wants you to be whole more than you do. He desires for you to walk in strength and peace, and He has given you a way to live it out. God desires for us to keep a soft and pliable heart towards Him, so

He can do with us what He needs us to do. His desire is to make us into a vessel that can be used for His glory alone.

Allowing God to Mold You

Have you ever made the statement, "I'll never do that? I could never travel to Africa or get up and speak or witness to a stranger or…"

I believe that if you make those types of definitive statements about what you're willing to do or not do, your heart isn't soft towards God. I've found myself many times making those declarations only to find myself doing the very thing that I said I would never do. God calls us out of our little boxes so that He can make us whole. If we are making declarative statements about what we will and won't do, then perhaps we are not willing to do *anything* that God wants.

He might ask you to do those very things you said you'd never do, but with that type of attitude, would you even hear Him? If you're so set against doing a certain thing or being a certain way, then it would be wise to examine your heart. Chances are you're not willing to listen to the direction of the Holy Spirit!

Many times we build up walls around our hearts towards God and towards others. This makes it nearly impossible for us to examine ourselves in the light of the Word. In this case it doesn't matter what God might want, because we think that everything in us is okay, and if someone says that we're not okay, our defenses immediately go up. It's so important to stay humble in EVERY area of life, and like I mentioned, moldable. We are the clay and He is the potter. He knows what's best.

His plan for our lives is beautiful. We are safe in His hands, no matter what He chooses to do with us.

God has asked me to do so many things in my life that I thought were crazy. If I'm not willing to do these things, then I'm in disobedience and I'll never be free. I'll remain in bondage until I release my pride and say humbly, "Yes, Lord."

God loves us so much that He wants us to live a life that's free. Do you get it? Freedom is amazing! It's not being bound by a set of crazy rules, but having your heart so loved and focused on God that there literally is nothing we can't do. All of the dreams in our hearts, all the promises in the Bible...all of this is for us. Every bit of it. That's HIS desire for us, and it's not selfish in any way for us to agree with Him. He wants us to be whole in every area, free from hindrance.

Think about Esther and her life-threatening plea before the King, Ruth and her encounter with Boaz, David with Goliath, Abraham and Isaac, Moses and the Red Sea, Noah and the flood, Paul and the Gentiles...and the list goes on. They all were obedient and willing to follow God. Think about our perfect example, Jesus. On the eve of enduring the cross, He prays and cries out to God. He submits to the Father and lays down His own life.

In Luke 22:42 Jesus cries out, "Father, if you are willing, take this cup from me. Yet not my will, but yours be done." Jesus was willing to do anything, even give up His life. Jesus suffered a painful death so we could live in freedom and walk in full obedience to the Lord. If we're not walking in freedom, we're not living the life that Jesus laid down His life to give to us. We're not free to do everything He's called us to do. We're not whole.

Jesus died to set us free. When I started walking more fully in the freedom He's given to me, I noticed that I began giving of myself even more than I had before. I've been able to bless others more freely, minister with more power, and be more of the person whom God made me to be.

Even as a full-time vocational minister, I used to struggle with this. I always felt like I wasn't doing a good enough job or that I wasn't qualified. It's amazing that when we get things fixed on the inside of us, we are able to help others more. When we focus on our relationship with Christ, our outreach is much more enriched. It's necessary to be built up in order for us to effectively help others. Why would anyone be attracted to following Jesus if all of His followers are beaten down and discouraged while all the time living in brokenness and bondage?

Loving Unlovable Me

Have you ever been on an airplane? Before it takes off, the flight attendant goes through a short blurb about what you'd need to do in case of an emergency. One of the most important things they say is concerning the potential loss of cabin pressure. Read the following, referring to the oxygen mask that is released during this time.

> *Place it firmly over your nose and mouth, secure the elastic band behind your head, and breathe normally. Although the bag does not inflate, oxygen is flowing to the mask. **If you are traveling with a child or someone who requires assistance, secure your mask on first, and then assist the other person.** Keep your mask on until a uniformed crew member advises you to remove it.*

Secure *your mask on first*, then assist the other person. If we are always trying to help others without getting our own supply from the Lord, our help will simply be worldly wisdom – not to mention we will run dry and have nothing to give. How can we effectively love when we can't even love ourselves?

Beth Moore in her study "Breaking Free" mentions that she tried an experiment with a group of women that she was speaking to. This is what she says:

Not long ago I tried a little experiment as I spoke to a group of women on the subject of God's love. I asked them to look eye to eye with the person beside them and say, "God loves *me* so much." Almost instinctively they turned to one another and said, "God loves *you* so much." I stopped them and brought the switch in words to their attention.

We tried the exercise a second time and they were visibly uncomfortable. I asked why they were struggling with my request and many said, "I can easily tell the person next to me that God loves her, but I'm having a very hard time telling her that God loves me"[18].

This is one area where children have it right. They know they are loved. They know they're important. They don't even have to be told; they just know. A three year old understands that he is valuable and loved, even if others fail to show it properly. They have no problem accepting it. You'll never hear a small child say when complimented, "Oh, it was nothing..." They might not say anything, but they will gladly receive the compliment without any fight.

We are loved. We must know this deep down. God loves you. God loves me. In fact, I'm His favorite! The Word of God clearly shows us of His great love for us. If we don't believe it and can't love who God made us to be, then we don't believe God. Our opinion and definition of our *self* becomes more important than God himself. Since when did we ever know more than God?

Loving self comes down to knowing who you are in Christ. To know who you are in Christ means you must know what He says about you. To know what He says about you, you must read the word of God. I always believed things about myself that simply weren't true. They became part of my identity. I always thought I was shy, so I lived in fear of being around crowds. I never thought I was beautiful, so I dressed the part and never acted beautiful. I had confidence issues, so when I faced a situation to be confident, I would always buckle under the pressure. I felt like a failure, so I lived like what I had to say wasn't important because it didn't matter anyway. I had to go to the Word of God and redefine myself. I had to take the time to rid myself of the old ways of thinking and bring the new ones in.

This takes time, yes, but freedom is not free! It is a free gift from Jesus, yes, but walking it out and loving yourself for who GOD made you to be takes work...and it's worth every minute of it. I formed new beliefs specifically about who God made me to be, and I quoted them every single day for 30 days.

Even now when I start catching myself saying things that don't line up with God's word, I step back and change my words. I can't afford to let the enemy have one foot in the door, or he'll find a way to come in and take over. It's important to look at yourself in the mirror every day and say, "I love you! You are a beautiful masterpiece. God loves you so much...You're His!"

I guarantee a three year old could do it in an instant and would believe every word!

Jake (4): "Is that spider milk Mommy?"
Me: "Spider milk?? Ick, no."
Jake: "Then why are you pouring it down the sink?"
Me: "Because we didn't drink it fast enough and now it's expired."
Jake: "That's what I said, it's spider milk!"

Laurin, 2: "Mommy, my butt hurts... will you kiss my butt?

I took my 6 year old son to the pediatrician and after examining him the Doctor explained how she was going to swab his nose with a giant Q-tip and test his boogers for influenza. My son asked, "Could I just pick them instead?"

Chapter 10

Free to Be Held

As we were getting in the van & Zeke was buckled in his seat:

Zeke: *"Mom, let me hug your neck."*

Me: *"What, honey?"*

Zeke: *"Let me hug your neck!"*

Me: *"Okay!!"*

Zeke squeezed as hard as he could and we both started giggling. He pushed me back a little, grabbed my cheeks, and said, "Oh, Mommy, I wove you! I woooove you!!"

Most moms in the world have heard the same question asked time and time again: "Mommy, can you hold me?" Or the better version of the question is "hold you mommy, hold you?" On the other hand, there are some kids who never want to sit or be still until they crash after a long day of playing their hardest, but in most cases children seem to go through a stage where they want to be held. I know with my three kids every single one of them at some point have wanted to just sit for long periods of time with either me or my husband and be loved.

I was thinking about this earlier and was asked myself the question, "Why in the world do kids want to just sit in their parents' laps? Why, when there is so much else they could be doing, like playing with Barbie dolls or dinosaurs, writing on the walls, or so many other things, do they love to crawl up in my lap and just sit there?" It's not like I'm pouring out some great wisdom to a question they've asked or even playing a fun game with them during those times. They just like to be held. This simple act speaks volumes to my heart.

Many of us as adults don't seem to get this concept anymore. We feel that we've outgrown that desire, or we try to hide it. We feel like we're the strong ones now, and that we only need other people, or even God, when the times get tough and we can't handle it by ourselves. Even then, when we're in need of the greatest help, we still have a hard time asking others.

Children enjoy sitting and being loved. This shows a clear picture of our heavenly Father. They love being loved. They delight in Daddy's presence. They ask questions, and they are like little sponges, soaking up all that Daddy has to give. They understand naturally like Psalm 16:11 explains, "In your presence is fullness of joy." They find joy by just being loved and held. We, as children of God, can experience the same thing with our heavenly Daddy by just sitting and experiencing His presence.

Why Not Be Held?

Maybe we don't allow God to hold us because we're afraid. We don't know how to sit still. We think to ourselves, "Maybe He won't love me because I've messed up so badly." Sitting with God sometimes makes us face the reality of how much we need and depend on Him. It also causes us to face some of the hardships that have gone on in our lives head on. God wants to heal us deeply by His love, but so many times we are afraid of the pain. Afraid to face the hurts of the past. Afraid to drudge up and get rid of some of the "ugly" in us and let the love of God set us free to become who we are...so we hide behind work, and stay busy. We hide behind always spending time with others and our family. We'd rather fold the laundry or run the errands or even watch TV. We hide behind just about anything to keep from looking at God's loving eyes and pouring out our hearts to Him. That's what He wants. He wants us. Nothing more. I believe it's because we've forgotten how to simply be still with God or even with others. What is it with being vulnerable that is such a challenge for most of us? Why is it so difficult to let our guard down?

I know that over the course of my life many people have let me down and hurt me so severely that I never feel like I could ever be real with anyone again. Friendship has always been something that I place great value on. When you and I become close friends, don't be shocked if you are blessed because writing cards, giving gifts, and hanging out are things that I do best to show others that I care. These are all acts of vulnerability for me, and of course, sometimes they might not be received in the way that I hope. That's when I realize that maybe this person I'm reaching out to might not be ready to open up to me in return. Either way, I need to be obedient to do what God has called me to do and be willing to put myself out there to see if this might be someone God has put in my life to go deeper with.

My Best Friend Janet

At one time I had a good friend named Janet. Well, I considered Janet to be my best friend during this particular time of my life. I was married with 2 children at the time, and Janet and I would spend time together almost every day. We would go running together 3 times a week, and she'd come over for dinner on a regular basis. She was a great friend to the family and especially to me.

When situations changed in my life and God was calling my family to move, it got tough. She walked through that time with me, and honestly, moving away was very difficult for me. I knew that it was God's timing and His will for us to go, but it's not what I wanted to do. Leaving close friends is not easy.

We moved about an hour away, and I still maintained a great friendship with Janet. I'd go back and visit often, because that's where Chris's parents were from, and she and I would still talk most every day. I would certainly say that I was open with Janet. We'd spent so much time talking and hanging out, and I felt like I could trust her with a piece of my heart, as well as some of my deepest thoughts and emotions.

About a year after I moved away, it was time for Janet to move as well. She got a job in New York City, not close at all to where I was living in North Carolina. I offered to pack up my van and drive her there, so that's what we did. We loaded down the minivan with all of her living essentials and drove to her new apartment in NYC. After being there a day or two, it was time for me to drive home...and it wasn't easy. I probably was in tears half of the nine hour trip home because my closest friend was now so far away, and I knew that our visits would be few and far between. I knew that our friendship would change, but I wasn't prepared for what was about to take place.

After she moved, we continued to talk almost every day on the phone for the first couple of months that she was up there. At this time I was pregnant with my 3rd child, Stephen. Of course my emotions were all over the place, not to mention I still hadn't truly connected with anyone in my new home, so I began to feel lonely. One day, while having one of our normal conversations, Janet told me point blank that she didn't feel as if we should talk very much anymore and that she needed to make new friends where she lived. Needless to say I was taken aback, and it hurt me deeply.

I had no idea what happened, what I had done, or where our friendship was at that point. I knew that things were changing, but I felt that it was a bit drastic to just call the friendship off so abruptly. My heart was broken. I was hurting, and I couldn't understand why. I felt even more alone and very upset much of the time. I would cry out to God and ask Him to please heal my heart, to help me forgive Janet, and just to give me peace.

I would have to say that this period of time was one of the most difficult seasons in my life, even to this day. I mentioned that friends are important to me, and not having close friends was something that I was not used to. It was difficult for me to want to trust anyone else that God would bring to me, and not to mention, it was difficult to even trust myself anymore. I wasn't sure if I could handle a close friendship again, fearing that I would totally ruin it because of my insecurity and fear. I desperately needed God to heal my heart.

About a month after Stephen was born, we went on a cruise to Hawaii with my extended family. Since I was up anyway at 4 in the morning to feed my newborn on top of the fact that my body was used to Eastern Time, I would go out and watch the sunrise from the cruise ship deck. I went out, found a place to sit and literally cried out to Jesus because my heart still hurt so much. I wrote in my journal and just let the Lord love on me during that time. I'll never forget one morning when I was out there, God met me in such a powerful way. He touched my heart and made it new again…in an instant. At that moment I knew that everything was going to be okay. I was curled up in my Daddy's lap, and He loved on me and held me tight, like only He can do. He let me know that I didn't need to worry anymore, that His love is always sufficient for me, and that I am never, ever alone. If I didn't take the time to just sit with God and let Him love me, that healing in my heart would never have come. Allowing God into the deepest parts of your heart is such a vital part of healing and being whole.

Since then things have been different. God has brought many new friends in my path, and I am thankful. When I'm at a place to be vulnerable with a friend, now I lean on God knowing that no matter what happens He will take care of me…even if the friend doesn't respond like I want or feel like she should. I definitely have not mastered this area of my life, but I know that it is in God's best interest and in mine to continue to pursue new, deep, meaningful friendships.

Just so you know, about a year after all of the hardship happened with my friend, Janet, I received a letter from her. It was an apology for the way she handled things and it was obvious that God had moved powerfully in her life, just like He moved powerfully in mine. Neither of us was perfect in our friendship by any means, and both of us needed to forgive. God restored the friendship, we've forgiven one another and, truthfully, she'll always in my heart be one of my dearest friends. We don't talk or see each other very often, but when we do it's clear that God did His amazing work between us. He is so faithful!

To Love is to be Vulnerable

Learning how to be vulnerable in every area of my heart with Jesus empowers me to have the strength to be open and to be vulnerable with friends and family. People will always let you down, but then again, I let others down all the time too. Everyone needs others to help them get through life. Having close relationships is a wonderful blessing, and trying to protect ourselves from letting our guard down or the potential of being hurt allows Satan to steal away a gift that God is trying to give us. It displays a lack of trust in God when we refuse to be "real" with the friends that God has placed in our paths. Of course not every person you come across is someone that will be your nearest and dearest friend, but God undeniably puts a handful of people there for you to live life with on a deeper level.

Consider this quote from C.S. Lewis in "The Four Loves":

> *"To love at all is to be vulnerable. Love anything and your heart will be wrung and possibly broken. If you want to make sure of keeping it intact you must give it to no one, not even an animal. Wrap it carefully round with hobbies and little luxuries; avoid all entanglements. Lock it up safe in the casket or coffin of your selfishness. But in that casket, safe, dark, motionless, airless, it will change. It will not be broken; it will become unbreakable, impenetrable, irredeemable. To love is to be vulnerable.[19]"*

If someone hurts your heart in a friendship or any relationship, be careful not to allow that hurt to dictate the depth of future relationships. Let me reiterate that last part: be careful not to allow a past hurt in a relationship to dictate or to define the depth and vulnerability of future relationships. We must forgive and move past it, always TRUSTING that God has our best interests at heart. He always protects us, and if we're following His lead, we can give ourselves to others trusting that our heart is in the palm of His hand.

Can I just say how amazing it is to know that I have people I can trust to believe with me and pray with me when I'm going through a difficult time! It's such a wonderful thing to know that I have these types of friends in my life whom I can run to when I need encouragement and love - friends who display the love of Christ to me, even in the difficult times. These are the family members and friends who know the "real me," because I have chosen to let them into my life; the ones who love me even though they've seen my faults and many shortcomings.

Healing and Restoration

I am deeply thankful for these people, and I know that they have been and are a gift from God to me to make my life even more valuable. Sure, there are many difficult times in relationships where there might be confusion, hurt, disappointment, and even anger, but it's all worth it when you look at the incredible times and deep relationships that go along with it.

Have you ever noticed with kids that immediately after they've done something wrong and received discipline for it the very first thing they tend to do is come right back and love on the one who gave it?

They want mommy to hold them and love on them...even after a time of correction.

This is a wonderful part of the process of healing. During the act of discipline it is a time of complete vulnerability for them. They've been caught, realized that they've done something wrong, and need to be corrected for it. I believe that the moment after discipline is such a vital part for complete healing and restoration. It brings a closure to the entire process, and it doesn't allow it to end on a "bad note." It ends with a sense of love and security, showing the child that although they might have messed up, there is nothing that they can do that will cause them to be loved any less.

The same goes for us. If we've messed up in a relationship with someone there needs to be a time of restoration. We need to make sure that we reach out to the other person, whether we were the ones who were hurt or if we were the ones who caused the hurt. This is that same type of vulnerability that is shown when the children are facing discipline. It's not easy, but it's necessary for true restoration and healing to occur. If this step is overlooked or simply swept under the rug like, it allows for the hurt and the pain to sink down into our hearts. It's never officially dealt with, so it just gets buried.

When wound after wound gets swept under the rug, it eventually ends up with a relationship and a heart that is never free. Many times the parties will move on because it just "didn't work out." We need to make sure that we are ones who don't allow fear of vulnerability to take over and keep us from confronting others when it is necessary. Even if your friend is someone who might not like it, someone in the relationship needs to not be afraid to be open and vulnerable.

When you choose to step above fear and let your guard down, it opens the door for the other person to do the same. It empowers them to be free. Openness, vulnerability, and clarity are all things that a 3 year old is simply not afraid of. What an example for us they are!

One more important thought on this subject: God wants us to be wide open before Him. I know many times in life when I mess up I've felt like I've let God down as well as everyone else around me. I've felt so unworthy to be loved, and in return I don't allow anyone, including God to have the opportunity to love and encourage me. I don't let Him hold me because of a feeling of unworthiness. I didn't know how to receive love because I thought I didn't deserve it.

Even if someone would come and encourage me, I didn't accept it. After all, I failed and I should wallow in my failure, right? I messed up, so I should be punished and ashamed of what I did. NO! This attitude is so ungodly! Yes, when we mess up or fail, we should repent and make amends for it. Yes, we should apologize to whomever we did wrong, but when we've done our part to make it right, and as long as we're truly repentant, that should be the end of it. Just like when a child gets in trouble and is disciplined we need to run to the arms of God and let Him restore us.

The last thing we should do is roll around on the ground wallowing in self-pity for simply making a mistake — even if you think it's a big one. Satan gets the best of us when we do this, and the bad thing is that we think we're being holy by acting this way! God sent us His son so that through Him our sins are forgiven and we become worthy even when we've messed up. We repent and run to God and He brings us back immediately; Not after we've done something to impress Him again or performed our penance for the sin we committed. He gently corrects us and gets us back up on the path so that we can finish the race.

His desire is for us to run to Him and allow Him to show us time and time again that His love reaches way beyond any wrong that we can do or any wrong that we have ever done. It's this love and restitution that gives us the strength to do better the next time. The quicker we get up, the less time we spend down. God is so wonderful, and when we learn to accept His immediate forgiveness and run to Him like was mentioned in a previous chapter, we'll see our races becoming shorter and shorter because we're actually running instead of lying around on the ground, thinking we deserve this punishment!

God loves you. He adores when you sit in His presence and just talk to Him. He loves when you take walks with Him, pouring your heart out and letting Him show you how much He loves you. He enjoys being around you! He loves to hear what's on your heart and in your deepest thoughts. It's not that He doesn't know them already, but when you open up and share with Him it brings healing. It brings a new level of intimacy between you and your heavenly Daddy. Vulnerability and intimacy with God gives you the strength and the ability to trust being in a close relationship with others.

So the next time a child runs to you and wants to sit in your lap, remember our God and how He loves to know everything about you and how He loves to sit and hold you. No words are even necessary. Ask yourself if you've taken the time to sit in His lap lately and tell Him about your day. Have you taken the time to let Him hold you...or better yet, for you to hold Him? He's waiting for you with arms wide open and a great big smile on His face!

Stephen, age 7, was being interviewed by the pastor about his upcoming baptism. "What does death mean, Stephen?" To which Stephen replied, "It has two meanings. First, it means to die, and second, it means that you can't hear."

My ten year old daughter, Annie, accidently tripped and bumped into her four year old cousin, Mindy. Annie immediately said "I'm sorry Mindy I lost my balance." A few minutes later Mindy came running out of the bedroom saying "Annie look, I found your balance." Then she held out one of my New Balance tennis shoes.
(Heardontheplayground.com)

CLINTON (age 5) was in his bedroom looking worried. When his Mom asked what was troubling him, he replied, "I don't know what'll happen with this bed when I get married. How will my wife fit in?"(www.HeardonthePlayground.com)

Chapter 11

Free to Genuinely Connect

Melanie (age 5) asked her Granny how old she was. Granny replied she was so old she didn't remember any more. Melanie said, "If you don't remember you hafta look in the back of your panties. Mine say five to six." (*HeardonthePlayground.com*)

"Your love never fails, never gives up, never runs out on me." These are the lyrics from a very powerful worship song entitled *One Thing Remains*. Jesus' love never fails. He never gives up on us. He is always pursuing a relationship with us. No matter how many times we say no, He comes back, arms extended and ready to love us more than we could ever imagine.

Kids are the same way. If they want something, chances are you're going to hear about it at least once. Or twice. Or even three times. They won't let go. If you say you're going to do something for them, they will remind you until you do. I love that about them.

Children love and they connect. In fact, just about everything they do is based on their connection with others. They never give up on people. They love despite the odds, without expecting you to be a certain way in return. It doesn't matter how bad a situation is at home, children love their parents and their family unconditionally. They care about connection. Jesus does too. He does not condemn anyone. His whole desire is to be connected deeply with us because of His great love for us.

Picture this: you're sitting at a preschool Christmas program waiting for your child to come out on the stage. All the parents, grandparents, and friends have their cameras ready; videos are rolling and the anticipation is mounting.

Then the children appear from backstage all dressed up in their reds and greens, of course, ready to put on a great show for you. What's the first thing those children do when they walk out on stage? They don't think about impressing the crowd or even looking their best. They don't fix their hair or look in the mirror to make sure their makeup is on correctly. No. They are thinking about finding someone who is important to them.

The first thing they do is immediately look for their parents and wave. And when they spot us, a huge smile comes and their faces light up. And we do the same in return. We look for them and wave. We smile. They don't care if anyone else is looking or even if they look silly. They want to know their parents are there and they will do anything to show that connection. How does that make you feel as the parent? Amazing!

When you see someone you love cheering you on, or even when you're cheering someone on that you love, it is a priceless moment...and being connected feels so good.

We've talked a lot about vulnerability throughout this book. That's because children are so vulnerable. They have to be. They have not yet been taught to put up walls when they get hurt. They are not out to impress anyone, to look a certain way, or to develop some kind of false image. They are who they are, and they let it show. They put themselves out there for the world to see.

When my second daughter, Hope, was 3 years old, we had some guests over for dinner one night. They were new to the church, and we wanted to invite them over to get to know them better. In the middle of eating some melt-in-your-mouth pot roast surrounded by chunks of potatoes, Hope leans over to our friend, Lauren, and excitedly says to her, "I poopied a BIG one last night."

Of course Chris and I looked at each other and gasped in astonishment mixed with embarrassment, but it was hilarious. Everyone burst out laughing. No one who was at that table will ever forget that statement. Hope didn't care! She was just excited about something and felt the need to share. She definitely put herself out there!

Letting Your Story Be Seen

I've recently come across the work of a researcher named Brené Brown. She has done extensive study on the power of vulnerability and how it is necessary in life to lead a life full of fulfillment. She's been through life-changing experiences herself while studying this topic, realizing that vulnerability with others is the key to so many of the great things in life. After studying and interviewing thousands of people, she came up with some amazing conclusions about the power of vulnerability.

The definition that she found for the word courage was this:

Courage — to tell the story of who you are with your whole heart. The word courage is derived from the Latin *Cor* meaning heart.

"To tell the story of who you are with your whole heart." Now that is real courage. She even goes on to say that "the most accurate measurement of courage is vulnerability." In other words, if you're putting yourself out there, showing people your flaws, going for it when things seem tough, telling people you love them first, taking the first step, letting others into your heart and life, etc., then you're considered courageous, and I totally agree with her!

In her multiple years of research and interviews among thousands of people, she has come to this conclusion: "Connection is the reason we're here." It gives purpose and meaning to our lives. Shame, which we talked about in a different chapter, is why we don't let ourselves be seen in a deep way by others. Shame says, "I'm not good enough," or I'm not ___ enough, which keeps us from allowing our true self to be seen by others. Shame, as she defines it, is the fear of disconnection.[20] Therefore, if we allow shame to rule our lives, we remain, for the most part, disconnected with those around us, and that steals a great deal of the joy and freedom Christ has to offer.

How many times have you wondered, "Why on earth am I here? What is this life all about?" Many times I feel this way. I feel hopeless and wonder what in the world am I doing. Am I making a difference? Why did you put me on this earth, Lord? I absolutely believe this is the answer.

We are here to be connected — first to God, then with those around us. We are divinely designed to need this, and it's placed deep within our souls. It is why we are here. Being in relationship with God and with others is more important than anything else on this planet. Anything. He has created us to connect deeply, and if we don't, our lives won't be as meaningful, and we will always feel as if something is missing.

Brown goes on to divide people into two different categories. The ones she deems wholehearted: those who have a strong sense of love and connection; and the ones who are not wholehearted: those who aren't deeply connected with others. She then goes into extensive research on why people fall into the category that they do. It boils down to this: the ones who have a strong sense of connection believe that they are worthy of love and connection. The ones who do not, don't believe that they are worthy of love and connection.[21] It's that simple.

You have to remember that Brene Brown is not an outspoken Christian researcher. She came to these conclusions based on her secular research, and what she discovered is exactly what God had in mind from the very beginning! He wants to connect with us! Jesus died on the cross for one reason - so we can be connected with the Father. Without Jesus we could never come to Father God. Even from the very beginning, God created Adam and Eve for what purpose? To love Him. To be in fellowship with Him. When they sinned it broke their fellowship with God.

When He comes into our lives, not only are we worthy, we are made whole! We are granted the ability to enter into a deep, intimate relationship with the

Creator of the universe! Our relationship with Him is like any other relationship in that it takes time.

Just because you believe in Him and have now been introduced to Him doesn't mean that you are immediately deeply connected. That part takes time and effort. He is always there waiting for you to come to Him. He desires intimacy with you much more than you ever could with Him. He is the one who knows our hearts and loves us the same. The one who sets us free. Free to be who He uniquely created us to be. Free to deeply love Him!

Through her extensive research, Brown came to the conclusion that those who are wholehearted embrace being vulnerable. They have a deep connection with others as a result of being authentic or real. They are willing to let go of the thought of who they should be in order to be who they are.

The wholehearted have the courage to be imperfect. What makes them vulnerable makes them beautiful. The willingness to say I love you first, to do something where there are no guarantees, to invest in a relationship that may or may not work out, it's fundamental to them. It's part of what they do, even though it might hurt sometimes.[22]

Those who are wholehearted are willing to let themselves be seen. They put themselves out there, not concerned with what anyone else thinks. They are willing to take wise risks in faith that God has them in His hands, even if it could end up in pain. All of these are important for intimacy and connection with others, not to mention to see our dreams fulfilled in our lives!

Let me pull one of the statements out from a previous paragraph and address it here. Brown mentioned that the wholehearted are willing to let go of the thought of who they should be in order to be who they are. What makes them vulnerable makes them beautiful. What we've experienced in life, all of our failings, our problems, our hurts, our pain, and our mistakes...all of these things have been used by God to form us into who we are.

All of our bad choices or things we think we should regret have impacted our lives, and because of God, we are better for it. We are not defined nor are we limited by our past, but as we are vulnerable with our past by allowing God to use it, our past has the ability to propel us into all that God has for us in our future. Romans 8:28 says, "And we know that in all things God works for the good of those who love him, who have been called according to His purpose."

As we embrace and confront our mistakes, pains, fears, and failures while releasing the shame, we become even more of who God made us to be. As we show ourselves to those around us and use our past as a testimony for His glory; the impact we will have for the kingdom of God and others will be huge.

God will allow us to connect not only on a deeper level with Him, but showing our true selves, even the "bad" parts, allows us to embrace who we are, and it gives God permission to take our old lives and transform the bad into the beautiful. It also gives others permission to embrace us deeply as well. Being vulnerable with what we think makes us ugly, actually propels us into a beauty that is beyond compare. Wow!

Who are We?

So who are we, really? I've wrestled with this a lot as I've been writing this chapter. Our lives are not our own. We are God's. We are not limited or even defined as a person by what happened in our past; however, our past has molded us and shaped us to be who we are…good or bad, of course until God gets His hands on us.

A quote from Francis Frangipane in the book *The Three Battlegrounds* addresses this truth quite well:

> *In addition to the mind, the will and the emotions, our soul is made of events and how we reacted to those events. Abuses and afflictions hammer us one way, encouragement inflates us another. Our reaction to each event, whether it was positive or negative, is poured into the creative marrow of our individuality, where it is blended into the nature of our character. Although the events of our lives are irreversible, our reactions to those events can still be changed. As we change our reactions to the past, we change. In other words, although we cannot alter the past, as an act of worship, we can put our past upon the altar.[23]* — The Three Battlegrounds

We are who God says we are, not what the world says. I've always had a mentality that we should overcome our past, but that's not the truth at all. We can't change what happened, but we must face it and accept it. It is a part of who we are. That's just a fact. There is no shame in that. We should, however, overcome the ungodly beliefs we formed during those times and change them into godly beliefs. It's also wise to look at what happened and learn from it. Allow God to use it fully to minister to Him and for Him.

Until we accept our past and look at it through God's eyes, we will never be able to be vulnerable about our lives with Him or with others, and therefore we will not be able to connect deeply. Our past has been forgiven completely if we have allowed Christ into our hearts — no more shame and no more hiding.

This is how true connection with others happens. This is why we were created. This is the reason we exist...to connect with God. To relate to him with deep intimacy. To connect with the people God has created. To love beyond ourselves. To show each other who we really are and to love others in spite of their failures and their faults. To be there for one another, and as Galatians 6:2 says, "To bear one another's burdens...." We were made to connect.

I find it amazing how God can take something that is so horrible in our lives and turn it into something so beautiful. How can He take something so painful and make it into a place of beauty? How can He take our mistakes and turn them around for His glory? How can He love someone like me who is flawed beyond belief? How?

He is love. God is love. It's not something He does, it's who He is, and He lives inside of us. We were created for Him. We were created to love deeply and be deeply loved. It is an amazing feeling and experience to love and to connect deeply.

When I look back on my life of thirty-something years, all of the wonderful memories have been moments I've shared with others—with close friends, family members, church family, and especially with Jesus. Moments of uncontrollable laughter, fun, deep conversations, and yes, even tears. There have been so many of these amazing times in my life and I am so thankful for them. My heart has been full of the love of Christ countless times. There is nothing in this world that can even come close in comparison to the love of God filling my heart. Sometimes that happens when I'm alone with Him, other times it's when I'm with those close to me.

Sadly, the difficult and painful memories have also been ones involving the people I deeply love—even with God himself. Though God has never done anything wrong, I've been hurt before, because He didn't do something the way I thought He should have.

Hear this. With deep connection comes deep pain. We are all fallen people, and no one on this earth loves perfectly. But through it all, we must remain committed to the reason we were placed on this earth. We must remain committed to Jesus and to each other through the pain.

Just because something might hurt doesn't mean we should avoid it. Just because your friend may have said something painful doesn't mean you drop the relationship. That's going to happen in any close relationship! It's usually through those relationships that the most growth in your personal life occurs. Just because people are imperfect doesn't mean you shouldn't reach out and love deeply.

C.S. Lewis puts it best: "When you love deeply, you're going to get hurt badly. But it's still worth it."

Take Jesus for example. He loves perfectly. He is a perfect example for us to follow. When He walked this earth He was deeply connected to God. He would spend days upon days fasting and praying. He would go out to the garden and pray while His disciples were sleeping. He was always in fellowship with God. Yes, He is God, but when He walked this earth He was 100 percent human. If He wasn't completely human, then why would He need to pray anyway?

Jesus was connected to God first, and then everyone else. He was always pouring wisdom into His disciples. He taught them what this life was all about. They left everything they knew to follow Him...to be connected to the Son of God. And He left everything and chose to die for us so that we could be connected to Him. He loved His disciples without measure. He called them friends. He opened up His life to them.

In John 15:15 Jesus says this: "I no longer call you servants, because a servant does not know his master's business. Instead, I have called you friends, for everything that I learned from my Father I have made known to you."

The disciples knew Jesus intimately. Can you imagine how deeply it cut when Judas betrayed Jesus? Can you imagine the pain Jesus experienced when Peter denied him three times? Indeed they were very close, and that is exactly how Jesus created us to be.

Not only was Jesus connected with His disciples, He had an impact on everyone that came across His path. Everyone loved Him and wanted to be around Him. He genuinely loved them. He reached out to them. He touched others, healed them, fed them, ministered to them, and gave His life for them. His life was all about loving people. He wasn't afraid to get close. He didn't keep His distance from anyone. He is our example of loving others. He loves without expecting anything in return.

I am someone who loves deeply. Honestly, sometimes I wish I didn't, because I've been hurt so many times in doing so. Most of the times, it's been because of unfulfilled expectations, but sometimes it's just because people are people and they aren't perfect. Loving deeply, connecting, and putting yourself out there hurts. But honestly, it's also the best feeling ever. It allows me to continue to love more like Jesus does. Even when others let me down, I will love them and do everything in my power to show them the love of Christ. Love never fails.

So many remarkable people are in my life right now simply because I was willing to put myself out there. I felt a nudge by the Lord a few years ago to ask my son's preschool teacher to have lunch one day. Not necessarily the typical thing to do, but I did. If I'd have been afraid, our lives would not be where they are now.

Not only did that preschool teacher become one of my dearest friends, God connected us with her church family and we have been accepted and loved by them like we've never experienced in a church before. God has given me many deep friendships through that one connection, not to mention a fellowship of believers who deeply love God, and I'm incredibly thankful. I'm so glad I sent that email asking for a lunch date. Because of it, my life has been totally changed.

God has been teaching me to love without any strings attached. I find it kind of ironic that we should love without strings attached yet be connected with others deeply. How do you connect with others when you shouldn't expect anything in return? Somehow children do.

Remember the illustration in the beginning? They are waving and smiling at you, making sure you're there. That's what God desires from us — to be looking for Him everywhere we go. To acknowledge Him in every facet of our lives. To always cast him a glance, a smile, or something that shows him that He's the most important one in our lives. To go about our day constantly thinking about the one who is so in love with us. He is always thinking about us. That's what He wants more than anything. He wants you. Your heart. Your trust. Your smile. You. You don't have to do anything to earn this love, and what a deep committed love it is. For eternity. No strings attached.

So let me challenge you...follow Him with everything you've got. Love Him with all your heart...and live free like you're three!

Group or Individual Study Questions

Chapter 1 questions—*Free to be Beautiful*

1. When *you* look in the mirror, what do *you* see?
2. Have you ever felt trapped in life, trying to escape and find joy, but unable to? If so, what did you do or are you doing to become free?
3. Why do you think you feel/felt this way?
4. What is your definition of beauty?
5. Does your appearance ever play a part in your confidence? Has it ever kept you from doing something you know you should have but you didn't because of the way you look?
6. Do you *know* you're beautiful?
7. Take some time and ask God about how you view yourself and what role it plays in your life.

Chapter 2 questions—*Free to be Me*

1. How do you deal with control? Are you someone who always needs to feel in control or are you at peace knowing God is in control?
2. In thinking about the Shame, Fear, Control, cycle, is this something you've noticed in your life? If so, how do you think God wants you to overcome it? Give an example.
3. How are you doing defining who you are in Christ? Do you try to live up to the world's standards or do you live free in the person Christ made you to be?
4. List some traits you have that are like Jesus.
5. List some traits you've lived by that are not from Jesus. Where do you think these came from?
6. Is there something you're holding onto, like the girl in the story, when you believe God has something so much more for you?
7. Spend some time and ask God about where you incorrectly define who you are.

Chapter 3 questions—*Free to be Perfectly Imperfect*

1. Jesus was fully human when He walked the earth. Do you realize that he lived a perfect life when He was on the earth? What do you think that looks like according to Biblical standards?
2. Do you understand what it means to be perfect in Christ? Do you believe that if you are saved you are already made perfect?
3. How can this realization in your life help you live free and in the power of the Holy Spirit?
4. Do you fall into the trap of making "perfect" rules for yourself and when you don't meet them you feel discouraged? Do you ever impose your "rules of perfection" on others? How do you think this makes them feel? How would it make you feel?
5. Do you find yourself "hiding behind serving" much like Martha did to avoid real, deep interaction with others?
6. If so, how can you change this?
7. Ask God how you can let go of your incorrect definition of perfection. Ask God to reveal how He's already made you perfect through Christ.

Chapter 4 questions—*Free to Dream Big*

1. Do you still have dreams for your life, or have you allowed other circumstances and/or distractions held you back from pursuing them?
2. Do you believe and know that God wants you to fulfill the dreams and desires He's placed in your heart?
3. What are some of the dreams that God has placed in your heart?
4. Are your dreams God-sized dreams, bigger than you can imagine?

5. What are some things you can practically do now to start pursuing all that God has placed in your heart?
6. Ask God to put new, God-sized dreams in your heart and don't be afraid to share them with others. Write them down and pray for wisdom for moving towards them.

Chapter 5 questions—*Free to Completely Trust*

1. Where in your life do you have the most difficulty trusting God?
2. The question is asked in this chapter, "How do trust Him completely to take care of every are of your life?" The author answers that question with this answer: "You get to know Him." How do you think this helps your dependence and trust in God?
3. How do you really get to know God in this intimate way?
4. How have circumstances in your life caused your trust in Christ to become shaky?
5. How can we fight discouragement and fear and trust God when our circumstances are completely going the opposite direction?
6. Do you believe it's possible to trust God like a 3 year old trusts her parents?
7. Take time to pray about where God might be asking you to trust Him more.

Chapter 6 questions—*Free to Forgive*

1. How do you define forgiveness?
2. One way the author defines forgiveness is basically saying "You don't owe me anything." Do you ever feel like someone owes you something?
3. Do you feel justified in negative actions towards someone when they don't meet your expectations?
4. Do you ever have a right to hold a grudge?

5. What do you think Jesus meant in Matt. 6:14-15 when He said "If you do not forgive men their sins, your Father will not forgive your sins?" What does that mean for a Christian?
6. Time heals all wounds. Actually time buries all wounds unless forgiveness has taken place. Are there any wounds from people in your past you have not forgiven that you need to deal with?
7. Ask God to clearly show you people or groups that you haven't truly forgiven. Ask Him to give you strength to forgive them and let go.

Chapter 7 questions—*Free to Ask*

1. When you need help, do you normally try to do it yourself, or do you feel free to ask others?
2. Do you ask God when you're in need, or do you usually try to figure things out by yourself?
3. Have you ever found yourself or are you in a season or place in life where you know you wanted to change but felt powerless to do so? What did you or are you doing to gain victory?
4. Think about this statement: "Thinking you're unworthy of forgiveness is actually a major form of pride." Can you explain why? Also, have you ever felt this way?
5. Do you think asking for forgiveness over and over again is the same as trampling on the grace of God? What do you think is the difference?
6. Take time to ask God for something great. Ask him to move in ways you cannot fathom and expect to see Him move!

Chapter 8 questions—*Free to Cry*

1. Would you describe yourself as a crier, or someone who does their best not to show emotion?

2. What does it mean to you to be broken?
3. Has God ever used a time of brokenness in your life to draw you closer to Him? If so, explain.
4. Being vulnerable with God and others sometimes is challenging. Why do you think it is important to allow others, especially God, to see your emotion?
5. God is a comforter to those in need of comfort. He tells us to "comfort those with the comfort we have received." (2 Cor. 1:4) Has God ever ministered through a friend to you with His comfort? Have you ever been the comforter for someone else?
6. Take a moment and ask God where He might be challenging you in being vulnerable with others.

Chapter 9 questions—*Free to Love the Unlovable*

1. How are you at loving people who are different from you?
2. Do you ever find yourself judging others because of the way someone dresses or even how they keep their home?
3. In your own words, what does it mean to be whole?
4. Have you ever made the statement, "I'll never do that!" Are you open to do *anything* God might call you to do?
5. Do you often overlook yourself in order to serve others?
6. Do you make sure to take time regularly to build yourself up before trying to help everyone else around you?
7. Ask God how you can love not only others around you more fully, but also love and take care of yourself in a better way.

Chapter 10 questions—*Free to be Held*

1. How would you describe your "being held" time with the Lord? Great? Ok? Or I really don't know how to just sit and let God love me?
2. In relationships do you let others see the real you, or do you tend to put up walls so you don't get hurt?
3. If you put up walls, what do you think from your life caused you to be this way?
4. Has your heart ever been broken? If so, what did you do to overcome it? Did you deal with it, or did you just let time "heal" it?
5. Do you have people in your life that you can be completely open and honest with? Do you have someone besides your spouse that you open up to and pray with?
6. Pray and ask the Lord if you have any walls that you've placed in your life keeping you from being completely open with others. Talk to Him about how you might break these walls down in your life.

Chapter 11 questions—*Free to Genuinely Connect*

1. What do you think about courage being linked to how vulnerable you are? Is it courageous to let others know who you really are?
2. "Brown goes on to divide people into two different categories. The ones she deems wholehearted: those who have a strong sense of love and connection; and the ones who are not wholehearted: those who aren't deeply connected with others." Would you consider yourself to be wholehearted based on her definition? How did you come to your conclusion?
3. Do you have regrets?
4. Do you believe that no matter where you came from in the past, despite any choice you made, regardless of how bad you think you are, that God has used every single thing to form you into who you are today?

5. How do you love without strings attached, yet be deeply connected with others?
6. Overall, would you say you live a life of freedom?
7. Ask God what areas He wants you to break out of bondage. Ask Him to help you become free, like you're 3!

CONNECT with *Alicia V. Sharpe*

Please feel free to contact Alicia V. Sharpe via email at:
aliciavsharpe1@gmail.com

Or follow her blog on the web at
aliciavsharpe.blogspot.com

Facebook: Alicia V Sharpe (Alicia VanHaelst Sharpe)

Follow her on Twitter: @aliciavsharpe

Alicia V. Sharpe is available for speaking engagements upon request.

End Notes

1 www.dictionary.com, "Beautiful" definition

2 www.wikipedia.com, "Beauty" definition

3 Kylstra, Chester and Betsy, *Restoring the Foundations: An Integrated Approach to Healing Ministry Volume 2* (Proclaiming His Word, Inc, 2001).

4 Kylstra, Chester and Betsy, Restoring the Foundations: An Integrated Approach to Healing Ministry Volume 2 (Proclaiming His Word, Inc, 2001).

5 Author Unknown.

6 Dictionary.com, "Perfect" definition

7 Paramount Pictures movie "Morning Glory," copyright 2010.

8 Judges 6:36-39

9 Matthew 9:29

10 Matthew 25:21

11 Matthew 6:25-31

12 Psalm 37:25

13 www.dictionary.com, "Forgive" definition

14 unknown

15 Gurmeet.net, Three Stories of Forgiveness, http://gurmeet.net/spiritual/stories-of-forgiveness/

16 Author unknown.

17 Wilkerson, David R. The Cross and the Switchblade. Penguin Publishing, November 1986.

18 Moore, Beth. Breaking Free, Revised ed. Workbook. Lifeway Christian Resources, November 2009 pg 176.

19 Lewis, C.S., The Four Loves. Houghton Mifflin Harcourt, Reissue edition, November 1991.

20 Brown, Brene. TED talk, "The Power of Vulnerability." Houston TX. June 2010, TEDx Houston. www.TED.com.

21 Brown, Brene. TED talk, "The Power of Vulnerability." Houston TX. June 2010, TEDx Houston. www.TED.com.

22 Brown, Brene. TED talk, "The Power of Vulnerability." Houston TX. June 2010, TEDx Houston. www.TED.com.

23 Frangipane, Francis. The Three Battlegrounds. Arrow Publications, June 2006.